Built, Unbuilt and Imagined Sydney

Other titles of interest:

Geographic Information System for Smart Cities
Prof. TM Vinod Kumar and Associates

Metropolitan Governance: Cases of Ahmedabad and Hyderabad
Dr. Vinita Yadav

India's Urban Confusion: Challenges and Strategies
Edited by Dr. M. Ramachandran

Designing Better Architecture Education: Global Realities and Local Reforms
Dr Manjari Chakraborty

The Ekistics of Animal and Human Conflict
Rishi Dev

Water Conservation Techniques in Traditional Human Settlements
Pietro Laureano

The City Observed: Notes from an Uunfolding India
Pallavi Shrivastava

Built, Unbuilt and Imagined Sydney

Dr Anuradha Chatterjee

COPAL PUBLISHING GROUP
Inspiring a better future through publishing

Published by Copal Publishing Group
E-143, Lajpat Nagar, Sahibabad,
Distt. Ghaziabad, UP – 201005, India

www.copalpublishing.com

First Published 2015
© Copal Publishing Group, 2015

This book contains information obtained from authentic and highly regarded sources. Reprinted material is quoted with permission. Reasonable efforts have been made to publish reliable data and information, but the authors and the publishers cannot assume responsibility for the validity of all materials. Neither the authors nor the publishers, nor anyone else associated with this publication, shall be liable for any loss, damage or liability directly or indirectly caused or alleged to be caused by this book.

Neither this book nor any part may be reproduced or transmitted in any form or by any means, electronic or mechanical, including photocopying, microfilming and recording, or by any information storage or retrieval system, without permission in writing from Copal Publishing Group. The consent of Copal Publishing Group does not extend to copying for general distribution, for promotion, for creating new works, or for resale. Specific permission must be obtained in writing from Copal Publishing Group for such copying.

Trademark notice: Product or corporate names may be trademarks or registered trademarks, and are used only for identification and explanation, without intent to infringe.

ISBN: 978-93-83419-16-6 (hard back)
ISBN: 978-93-83419-17-3 (e-book)

Typeset by Bhumi Graphics, New Delhi
Printed and bound by Bhavish Graphics, Chennai

Contents

Chapter 01   Architecture on Show   1

1.1	Introduction	2
1.2	Constructing Ornament	3
1.3	Interactive Surfaces and Modelled Environments	6
1.4	Real Needs, Imagined Solutions	9
1.5	Revolutions and Evolutions: Contemporary Japanese Architecture on Show	11
1.6	Urban Resonances: Two Exhibitions at Customs House Sydney	14
1.7	Living in the Ruins	17

Chapter 02   Talking Point   23

2.1	Introduction	24
2.2	Small Spaces, Big Ideas	25
2.3	'Form follows Flow'	27
2.4	Talking House	28
2.5	Culture of Criticism	30
2.6	Talking (up) the City	32
2.7	Spatial Intelligence and New Domesticities: TEDxSydney 2012	35
2.8	Building Sites: Weiss/Manfredi's Utzon Lecture at UNSW	36

Chapter 03   New Public Domains   41

3.1	Introduction	42
3.2	A 'Field Approach': Winning Scheme for Green Square Library and Plaza Design Competition	42
3.3	Urban Protocols	46
3.4	Sydney's New Downtown Central Park	48
3.5	Light Rail: Adaptive Reuse of Transport Infrastructure	50
3.6	Taylor Square: Sydney's First Bicycle Hub	53

| Chapter 04 | Immersive Installations and Public Art | 57 |

4.1	Introduction	58
4.2	Memory Room and Psychological Space	59
4.3	Communities in/of the Cloud	61
4.4	In-animate: Philip Beesley's Hylozoic Series: Sibyl	64
4.5	Healing Colours and Geometries: Edgecliff Medical Centre	67
4.6	Immersive Space of Imagination: LAVA's 'Other Worldly' Martian Embassy	71
4.7	Hovering Immaterially: Halo in Chippendale Green, Central Park Sydney	73
4.8	Public Art in Sydney's Taylor Square: Historical Imageries	75

| Chapter 05 | Ideas: Sites, Sights, and Visions | 79 |

5.1	Introduction	80
5.2	N: Speaking in Different Voices	81
5.3	Women and the Other Domains of Architectural Production	82
5.4	Spatial Narratives and Deviant Conditions	85
5.5	Imagining Other Cities: Super Sydney	88
5.6	Rural Habitat	90

| **Index** | | **98** |

Introduction

Built, Unbuilt, and Imagined Sydney presents the expanded field of architecture. It aims to show that the practice of architecture exceeds the work legally defensible under the title of the architect. Besides the design and construction of buildings, the disciplinary field of architecture consists of exhibition and display; discussions and lectures; competitions and visions of new public domains; interactions between art and architecture in the form of installations, performances, and public art; and ideas on new directions for the practice of architecture. The book, therefore, places emphasis on practice as an intellectual activity, in addition to the definition of the term informed by business and legal parameters. It is seen as the meaningful exercise of social, political, and critical knowledge, skills, and mindset in an urban, spatial, and tectonic condition. The practice is also a public act, mediated, legitimated, and made meaningful through its articulation in various institutional, public, and mediatic realms. The book focuses on built and unbuilt works (residential, commercial, interiors, and so on) in Sydney, inclusive of public art, object or furniture design, key invited or public lectures, studios, current projects in making, competitions, collaborations, exhibitions, installations, and outreach work. The focus is on the innovative and the original—not the ordinary or the purely commercial.

Built, Unbuilt, and Imagined Sydney is structured into five chapters: (1) Architecture on Show; (2) Talking Point; (3) Competitions and New Public Domains; (4) Immersive Installations and Public Art; (5) Ideas: Sites, Sights, and Visions. Unlike conventional scholarship on contemporary architecture or a monograph approach which could have focused on a city, a region, an architect, a period in history, the book employs a different literary form. The independent essays within each chapter derive from their origin as blog posts in World Architecture News, UK. The significance of this is that it aims to capture the effect of architecture media (print and online) in the new millennium. The speed of information exchange and flow is almost overwhelming to the point that narrative, sequence, and boundaries of knowledge are lost and blurred. The notion of currentness is much more narrowly conceived now, as knowledge is quickly produced as well as made obsolete. As a result, the essays are noticeably episodic as well as topical. The aim is, therefore, to demonstrate the vitality and intensity of architectural thought. Since, no media will satisfy the desire for wholeness or permanence, the book tries to pick out the critical and creative DNA of the city as well as the desires, affinities, and positions that are shaping the built environment, at least in Sydney.

The collection of essays reveals that all or most architects either adopt as their own or have an interest in an(other) field, such as art, urbanism and landscape, virtual reality and three-dimensional imaging, installation and lighting design, and so on. The collection of essays aims to reveal therefore the multidisciplinary, urban orientations, and fluid forms of practice.

Acknowledgements

I would like to thank the individuals, practices, and organizations who have been featured in the book and/or who have contributed variously through discussions, texts, and images of their works. A special thanks also needs to be conveyed to the editorial team at COPAL Publishing for their patience and guidance through this process. And finally, I would like to thank my colleagues and friends in Sydney, who were always convinced that it was a good idea to write this book: Jennifer Kwok, Davina Jackson, Chris Bosse, Patrick Keane, and Chris Johnson.

Figures

Figure 1 Maret Kalmar, Elements (sterling silver, 9ct gold, rubber) [Photo: Adrian Hall Photography]

Figure 2 Ksenija Benko (sterling silver, 9ct gold, rubber) [Photo: Adrian Hall Photography]

Figure 3 Michael Ripoll, Lonely Terrace (in sterling silver, copper, and ebony) [Photo: Michael Ripoll]

Figure 4 Robin Phillips, Walt Disney Concert Hall 1, after Frank Gehry (sterling silver) [Photo: Robin Phillips]

Figure 5 Hypersurface Architecture, Media Wall [Photo: Peter Murphy]

Figure 6 Hypersurface Architecture, Halo Wall, Customs House Forecourt [Photo: Peter Murphy]

Figure 7 Parallel Nippon [Photo: Anuradha Chatterjee]

Figure 8 Parallel Nippon [Photo: Anuradha Chatterjee]

Figure 9 People Building Better Cities [Photo: Peter Murphy]

Figure 10 Next Stop: 21st Century George Street [Photo: Peter Murphy]

Figure 11 Installation View, Room 1B, Living in the Ruins [Photo: Alex Davies]

Figure 12 Installation View, Room 1F, Living in the Ruins [Photo: Alex Davies]

Figure 13 Fabacus 1964 (First Australian Bank's Accounting Computer Used in Sydney) computer panel, installed in Sydney, manufactured by General Electric, 61 × 72.5 × 13.5 cm, on loan from The Westpac Banking Group Archives [Photo: Alex Davies]

Figure 14 Mordant Wing, Museum of Contemporary Art, Sydney [Photo: Anuradha Chatterjee]

Figure 15 Mordant Wing, MCA, Foyer Level 1, Looking out towards Circular Quay [Photo: Anuradha Chatterjee]

Figure 16 Urban Conversations Talk, Professor Edward Glaeser, Image courtesy NSW Department of Planning & Infrastructure, [Photo: Paul Wright]

Figure 17 Urban Conversations Panel, Image courtesy NSW Department of Planning & Infrastructure [Photo: Paul Wright]

Figure 18 Green Square Library and Plaza, View from Botany Road looking east to the Entry Triangle and Library Tower, Project: Stewart Hollenstein with Colin Stewart Architects [Image: Luxigon]

Figure 19 Green Square Library and Plaza, View from an adjacent apartment looking down over the plaza, Project: Stewart Hollenstein with Colin Stewart Architects [Image: Luxigon]

Figure 20 Memory Room [Photo: Tim da Rin]

Figure 21 Memory Room [Photo: Tim da Rin]

Figure 22 Cloudscape, Sydney Harbour, Vivid Sydney Festival 2012 [Photo: David Stefanoff]

Figure 23 Cloudscape, Sydney Harbour, Vivid Sydney Festival 2012 [Photo: David Stefanoff]

Figure 24 Hylozoic Series, Philip Beesley, Cockatoo Island, Sydney, The 18th Biennale of Sydney, 2012 [Photo: Anuradha Chatterjee]

Figure 25 Hylozoic Series, Philip Beesley, Cockatoo Island, Sydney, The 18th Biennale of Sydney, 2012 [Photo: Anuradha Chatterjee]

Figure 26 Hylozoic Series, Philip Beesley, Cockatoo Island, Sydney, The 18th Biennale of Sydney, 2012 [Photo: Anuradha Chatterjee]

Figure 27 Edgecliff Medical Centre [Photo: Brett Boardman]

Figure 28 Edgecliff Medical Centre [Photo: Brett Boardman]

Figure 29 Edgecliff Medical Centre [Photo: Brett Boardman]

Figure 30 Martian Embassy (View from the Embassy toward the Classroom) [Photo: Brett Boardman]

Figure 31 Martian Embassy, Primary Ribs and Secondary Ribs Axonometric, LAVA

Figure 32 Martian Embassy [Photo: Brett Boardman]

Figure 33 Halo, Halo Opening, 14 August 2012 [Photo: Anuradha Chatterjee]

Figure 34 Halo, Halo Opening, 14 August 2012 [Photo: Anuradha Chatterjee]

Figure 35 Tom Rivard, Table of Contents, *Arcade 4 / Points of Departure: Migratory Evidence* 753 BC to 2018 AD

Figure 36 Alecia Downie, Theseus, *Arcade 4 / Points of Departure: Migratory Evidence* 753 BC to 2018 AD

Figure 37 Tom Rivard, Section, Floating Theatre, *Arcade 4 / Points of Departure: Migratory Evidence* 753 BC to 2018 AD

Figure 38 Biomass Stove, Trinidad Family House (Don Gregorio and Nicolasa), by Mobile Workshop Architects

Figure 39 Exterior, Trinidad Family House (Don Gregorio and Nicolasa), by Mobile Workshop Architects

Figure 40 Interior, Trinidad Family House (Don Gregorio and Nicolasa), by Mobile Workshop Architects

Chapter 01

Architecture on Show

Abstract: Architecture on Show aims to capture interesting and impactful public exhibitions in Sydney on architecture and the related disciplines, focusing on displays in Customs House Sydney, Japan Foundation Gallery, UTS Gallery. Exhibitions are always less about the final and known, and more about the contingent and the possible. In Sydney, as the exhibitions are planned across different institutional exigencies, they are marked by a rich yet shifting diversity of curatorial stances, curators and co-curators, managers, governmental and corporate partners, contributors, venues, audiences, and media. Never replicated and always new, the exhibitions demonstrate critical revisions and silent revolutions in the discipline.

Key words: Curatorial, exhibition, interactive

1.1 Introduction

Architecture on Show aims to capture interesting and impactful public exhibitions in Sydney on architecture and the related disciplines, focusing on displays in Customs House Sydney, Japan Foundation Gallery, University of Technology (UTS) Gallery (others being Object Gallery, more recently opened Verge Gallery and Tin Shed Gallery at University of Sydney, and non-gallery space environments like Tusculum and Surry Hills Library). Sydney witnesses an explosion in architecture exhibitions during the various festivals (Sydney Architecture Festival, Venice Biennale, and Vivid Festival) and at the end of year period in the three architecture schools, University of Sydney, University of New South Wales, and University of Technology Sydney.

The role of exhibitions in architectural discourse was established since the Museum of Modern Art New York showed International Exhibition of Modern Architecture curated by Phillip Johnson and Henry Russell Hitchcock in 1932, which set the architectural agenda of the time as well as popularised international style. In addition, exhibitions today seek to explore the future, provoke questions of current concern, and test/prepare ground for architectural and urban projects, speculations, and collaborations. Exhibitions also play a role in consolidating institutional identity and societal legitimacy. Nevertheless, exhibitions are always less about the final and known, and more about the contingent and the possible. As the exhibitions are planned across different institutional exigencies, they are marked by a rich yet shifting diversity of curatorial stances, curators and co-curators, managers, governmental and corporate partners, contributors, venues, audiences, and media. Never replicated and always new, the exhibitions demonstrate critical revisions and silent revolutions in the discipline.

Constructing Ornament captures the exhibition at Craft NSW gallery at the Rocks, which presents a rare glimpse into the minds of jewellery designers who consider the world of architecture and city building as their own, adopting imageries and associations with specific buildings and construction processes as they craft wearable objects. The chapter also discusses the two exhibitions I curated for the Sydney Architecture Festival—Inter-action at Customs House and BE X Section at University of New South Wales (UNSW). While the exhibition at UNSW demonstrated student orientations to global citizenship, and creative solutions to the needs of local communities, the one at Customs House emphasized the tacit connections and shared territories between architecture, city planning and urban design, virtual reality, 3D modelling, landscape design, digital design and installation.

Revolutions and Evolutions picks out the agility of architectural thought in Japan, which is marked by the exigent need to reinvent the meaning of architectural practice in the economic climate of financial crisis. *Urban Resonances* compares the twin exhibitions at Customs House (People Building Better Cities and Next Stop George Street). It shows that public participation and consensus building is not only valued but also necessary for gaining societal legitimacy and continued professional relevance and effectiveness. *Living in the Ruins* is an insight into an exhibition by UTS Art, and while it is not an architectural exhibition, it contains the possibility of rethinking the future of architecture exhibitions as material, technological, and hence cultural histories of the practice.

1.2 Constructing Ornament

Walking along the Historic Rocks precinct in Sydney, I was lucky to come across a lovely exhibition titled *Architextural*, at the Gallery of Arts and Crafts NSW (31 July to 19 August 2012). Curated by Michael Ripoll, the exhibition is of hand-crafted jewellery informed by various architectural inspirations. The exhibition featured the works by jewellers/artists Carolyn Delzoppo, Val Aked, Ksenija Benko, Beth Spence, Maret Kalmar, Rosanne Antico Hall, Mike Ripoll, Margaret Conway, Robin Phillips, Laura Haszard, June Higgs, and Ruth Kerrison. While the connection between architecture and fashion, and more recently wearable art has preoccupied design publications, jewellery holds a precious position in its relation to architecture. It is not just architects love and wear jewellery and partake in designing and making them but it is also "jewellers who cite architecture as an inspiration for their works (Cameron, 2010)." Furthermore, it is the tactility, the craft value, and the alchemical properties of materials that strengthen the connection between architecture and jewellery. Cameron suggests that it is also the 'products and the mechanics of structure' that jewellers find aesthetically 'engaging, even intriguing, and often instructive on a technical level (Cameron, 2010).'

The collaboration between Frank Gehry and Tiffany & Co. is well known. Other examples include HK+NP studio, a Vancouver-based jewellery design studio that 'utilizes techniques and forms derived from the architectural backgrounds of the partners, Hiroko Kobayashi and Neil Prakash' (HK+NP Studio) and Sydney-based collaborative, Venerari. What is sometimes absent though is the designer/maker's commentary of the built world. Ute Decker's Architectural Jewellery exhibited in the London Festival of Architecture 2012 explores the 'relation of ethics and aesthetics in artefacts and the built environment and the concept of "social beauty" in her work with recycled silver, fair-trade gold, and bio-resin (Decker, 2012).' Put in this context, *Architextural* is a great discovery, a seeming one off in Sydney.

Figure 1 Maret Kalmar, Elements (sterling silver, 9ct gold, rubber) [Photo: Adrian Hall Photography]

Figure 2 Ksenija Benko (sterling silver, 9ct gold, rubber) [Photo: Adrian Hall Photography]

Michael Ripoll (2012), curator and jeweller, notes that even though nature has served as the source of metaphors and inspiration for jewellers/ artists, the everyday occupation of constructed and interior worlds also informs the artistic imaginary. Conversation with Ripoll (2012) strengthens my initial view of the connections between the disciplines of architecture and jewellery making—both involve a careful selection of material, devising precise processes of joining materials with specific chemical properties, and achieving a specific finish. The exhibiting jewellers/artists adopt distinctive approaches that acknowledge international architectural icons, historical buildings, city, room, home, and gardens, as well as narratives and experiences connected to the built environment. Hence, it is not the copying of forms of iconic buildings but the acknowledgement of the unconscious, incidental, trivial, and experiential dimensions of the built environment that informs these jewellers/artists.

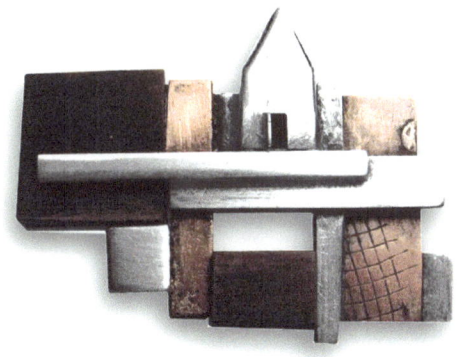

Figure 3 Michael Ripoll, Lonely Terrace (in sterling silver, copper, and ebony) [Photo: Michael Ripoll]

Figure 4 Robin Phillips, Walt Disney Concert Hall 1, after Frank Gehry (sterling silver) [Photo: Robin Phillips]

Site Lock Up and *Wrecking Ball* 1 by Kalmar (and number of other pieces, most of which are versions of necklaces) is a re-telling of her partner's experience of construction sites, as destructive, volatile, and unstable territories. Kalmar's *Birds that Lost their Tree* is a story of the removal of the bird's nest, containing within it a profound commentary on biodiversity. Ripoll's After *Mackintosh* focuses on the recognisability and scalability of the motif. While Ripoll's *Lonely Terrace* (in sterling silver, copper, and ebony) is a reflection of the Museum of Contemporary Arts in Sydney, which has received a lot of attention and criticism, the *Falling water* is a take on the overlapping planes created by Frank Lloyd Wright (Ripoll, 2012). Other recognizable icons are featured Robin Phillips's *Walt Disney Concert Hall 1, Frank Gehry* (sterling silver). Ripoll's *City of Man* presents the cityscape as overlays as do other works like Laura Haszard's *City*. Benko's *Elements* are a play on the geometric forms that must be negotiated in architectural compositions containing within it also the element of perspectival distortion. Ripoll's *Room with a View* is also about forced perspective. Cameron (2010) insightfully and accurately argues that '[v]iewing jewellery alongside architecture helps to reframe our viewpoint of jewellery practice, encouraging us to perceive our art form as a type of building practice; one concerned with the building of ornament.' *Architextural* is underpinned by the spoken and unspoken commentary on the built world by other disciplines and frameworks of imagination, and it is really encouraging to discover this hidden body of work.

1.3 Interactive Surfaces and Modelled Environments

As the guest curator for Sydney Architecture Festival, I directed the six exhibits under the aegis of the exhibition titled *Inter-Action* at Customs House in Sydney. The exhibition builds upon Customs House's profile in nurturing explorations in the fields of digital visualization and lighting technologies evidenced in past exhibitions such as *Form to Formless, Remodelling Architecture, Transclimatic,* and the Green Void, to name just a few. However, Inter-Action is not one but six exhibitions—*Hypersurface Architecture [Redux], Sydney from all Angles, Virtual Warrane II, Real/Virtual, Model City,* and *Open Agenda*.

The focus is on many disciplines (beyond architecture) that contribute to the making of the built realm. These include architecture, performance, art, and installation (*Open Agenda, Hypersurface Architecture*), architectural computing (*Hypersurface Architecture*), landscape architecture (*Sydney from all Angles*), web interface design (*Sydney from all Angles*), urban design, (*Model City*), digital visualization, and virtual environments (*Virtual Warrane II, Real/*

Virtual). The curation of the exhibitions needed to attend to the agendas and practices shared by these different disciplines. The key strands that emerge are: (1) Collaborative creation of knowledge, space, and experience; (2) Response to the city and its urban environment; (3) Crafting spatial and formal representations, both physical and virtual. The six exhibitions engage these strands in distinctive ways.

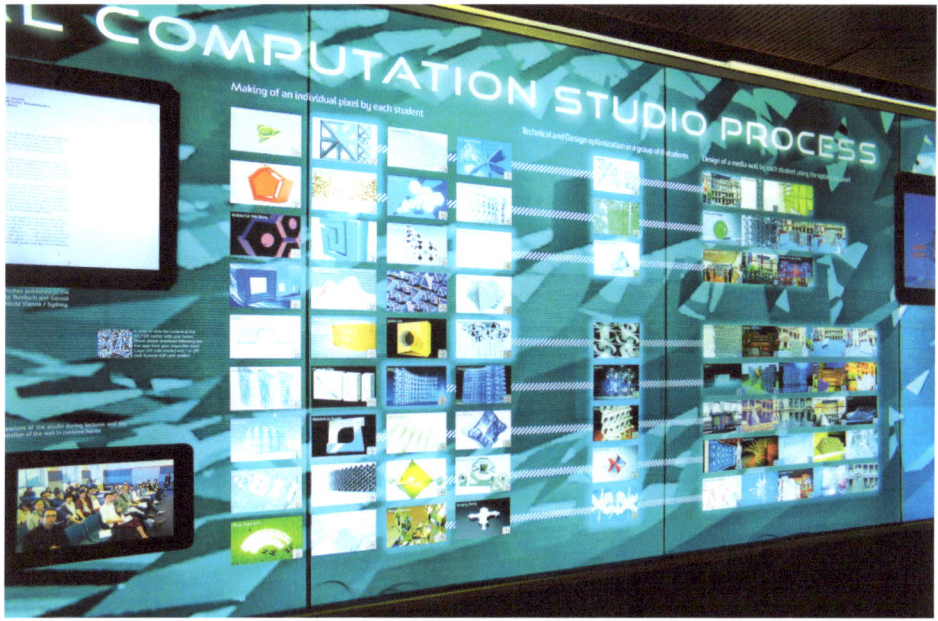

Figure 5 Hypersurface Architecture, Media Wall [Photo: Peter Murphy]

Hypersurface Architecture [Redux] is the design of an interactive media wall installation by Hank Hauesler and UNSW students and staff. It is composed of two walls—Halo Wall and the Euphonious Mobius—based on physical pixels, working thereby between the virtual and the real, attempting to "generate an 'infusion of form with media and media with form to work between the two" (Hauesler 2014). The installation is interactive as the movement of people is converted into data that informs varying intensities of light in the installations. The interactive aspect in *Sydney from all Angles* is achieved by embedding QR codes into a graphic map of Sydney, mounted on to the columns in the central void in the Customs House as well as glass floor covering the model of Sydney. The QR codes are linked to a website and recently designed key public domains, with the hope that people will continue to add their photos and stories to these public domains, thereby ensuring a continual and democratized engagement with as well as the curation of the experience of the public realm (Australian Institute of

Landscape Architects, 2012). *Virtual Warrane II* by Brett Leavy uses gaming techniques and technologies (complemented by solid archival research) to provide a way of inhabiting the past and participating in the landscapes of the Gadigal people, demonstrating constructed and built occupations prior to and underlying European settlement.

Figure 6 Hypersurface Architecture, Halo Wall, Customs House Forecourt [Photo: Peter Murphy]

The theme of modelling is explored further in *Real/Virtual* which compares miniaturization (city model), wire frame visualization, and stereo videos and panoramas of the city, highlighting technologies of visualization and different ways of creating navigable worlds. *Model City* is a display of physical models of key public precincts (under construction) in the City of Sydney, and it allows people to interact with the emerging public domains. *Open Agenda* (initiative of the School of Architecture, UTS) is an 'annual competition aimed at supporting a new generation of experimental architecture. Open to recent graduates, *Open Agenda* is focused on developing the possibilities of design research in architecture and the built environment (UTS, 2012).' The winning entries this year by Sibling, Tina Salama and Robert Beson explore other ways of conceptualizing architecture from participation to performative spatiality to the architectonics of atmosphere.

What started off as a challenge (bearing the risk of becoming eclectic), worked out to be a genuine opportunity. *Inter-action* preserved the identity of each exhibition, allowing the spatial opportunities inside Customs House to suggest rather than delineate synergies. In deploying different forms of interactive installations; modelled realities, pasts, and futures; and the speculation of the futures of architectural thinking, *Inter-action* celebrates the anticipation of the post-disciplinary in architectural thought. This is the emergence of new ways of knowing and doing, which is more than a simple convergence of different disciplinary knowledge systems.

1.4 Real Needs, Imagined Solutions

As the curator of BE | X-Section Real Needs | Imagined Solutions, the UNSW Built Environment's Exhibition for the Sydney Architecture Festival, it was interesting to showcase student projects from a range of Built Environment discipline degree programs that demonstrate shared awareness of social responsibility, collaboration, innovation, and most importantly an interdisciplinary knowledge base. These qualities, orientations, and attitudes contribute to the making of our UNSW Built Environment design students as intrepid graduates of global citizenship who understand and engage with the complexities of working with others in seeking creative solutions to real needs and issues identified by communities.

Real World

BEOutThere! electives capture the Interdisciplinary Service Learning in the Faculty of Built Environment, as they are carried out in collaboration with community partners with the expressed aim of exposing students to challenging social issues and considerations. In 2011 and 2012, key projects included: North Penrith Plaza—Designing a Digitally Enabled Public Domain; Northcott Project; Schools Project (Crown Street Public School, Ungarie Central School, and Tullibigeal Central School). The outcome and merit of these electives is the discernible and compelling nature of the interactions and the engagement evidenced in student reflections. Likewise, the significance of real world, industry-linked projects also informs *Integrated Low Carbon Living Project*. Delivered as a team-based collaborative project between students from BE and Faculty of Engineering students, the studio presents the opportunity to design the Material Science and Engineering Building, UNSW with attention to low energy, passive design strategies, design with zero net-energy and zero net-water consumption as the goal.

Social Inclusion

Student works in the *Socially Responsible Packaging* demonstrate a range of approaches to packaging—the liminal and the most intimate threshold between the user and the product. The projects address contemporary issues of safety, convenience, and access by synthesizing aesthetics, functionality, and ethical response. *Inclusive Architecture* progresses a similar argument that inclusive design (also known as universal design, design for all, user-centred design, human-centred design) 'is no longer a niche or unimportant endeavour.' Student projects which suggest inclusive redesigns of key 20th century buildings demonstrate that architectural merit is not irreconcilable with these goals.

Urban Orientations

The Intersection: Redevelopment of the SEU School of Architecture Building and its Landscape brings together students from three programmes (architecture, interior, and landscape) to make sense of the tectonic, landscape, and interior conditions of the Southeast University and the School of Architecture as a cultural and historical phenomenon, to inform redevelopment proposals. In contrast, it is the post-traumatic urbanist lens that informs the *Landscape Urbanism for the Shattered Garden City: Christchurch*. The fractures caused by natural disasters insert not only irreconcilable ruptures but also the opportunity for the new. Fittingly then, the students explore possibilities for city's open space system and for vitalizing that with the proposals for an urban arena with sport or performance facility, facilities for both having been extensively damaged across the city. Interior projects in the City of Sydney need to maintain an orientation to urbanism. *Taylor Square Bicycle Hub* is one such project, and the student projects demonstrate unique and meaningful approaches that seek translations of the figure of the bicycle as (1) a mechanical assemblage and meticulous orchestration of parts; (2) bicycle as generative of movement systems, motion, travelling, and energy; and (3) bicycling as a social sport that not only activates the urban area but also highlights the uniqueness of the site.

Generated by students in undergraduate and postgraduate programmes, the exhibition demonstrates shared commitment, knowledge systems, and capabilities. BE | X-Section reveals that unlike the technological, formal ingenuity and production orientation enabled and rewarded in many architecture and design schools across the globe, socially responsive design and architecture in its attention to authenticity emerges out of vital creative engagements between built environment designers and many people—it emphasizes intent over form, process over outcome, shared knowledge over individualistic expertise and action over representation.

1.5 Revolutions and Evolutions: Contemporary Japanese Architecture on Show

The Japan Foundation recently hosted a two-part exhibition *Parallel Nippon: Contemporary Japanese Architecture 1996–2006*, which featured over 100 large photo panels of designs, models, and video of projects recently completed by Japanese architects in Japan and overseas, between 1996 and 2006, including the works by Toyo Ito (winner of 2013 Pritzker Architecture Prize), KengoKuma, Tadao Ando, KenzoTange, SANAA, and many more. Curated around four themes of 'Urban Cycles: Centre and Periphery' and 'Life Cycles: Cradle to Grave' (Part One from 02 to 13 April 2013); and 'Culture Cycles: Environment, Information, Art' and 'Living Cycles: Conformity and Diversion' (Part Two from 17 April to 01 May 2013), *Parallel Nippon* sought to capture the revolutions and evolutions in the conceptualization and practice of architecture marking the changes in the post-recession social landscape of Japan, marked by challenges of urban migration, declining birth rate, aging population, and changes in family structure (Furuto, 2014). The catalogue essays by Riichi Miyake Professor of Architectural History at Keio University and Taro Igarashi Assistant Professor of Architectural History at Tohoku University shed more light on these issues.

Figure 7 Parallel Nippon [Photo: Anuradha Chatterjee]

Miyake notes: 'These years have seen structural changes in Japanese society in response to the shift from so-called "Bubble" to "Post-Bubble" economies; likewise, as policy making veered away from the 20th century expanding city toward a 21st-century continuous-city model, the move has been to effectively draw upon whatever attributes of long-standing heritage to the pursuit of new directions in value creation (Japan Foundation, 2013, p2).' Miyake suggests that the 'big, brash cultural monuments that aspire to world record stature" are obsolete, giving way to environments more attuned to the user, participatory design, and works connected to the finer urban grain (p2). Miyake presents the themes of Urban Cycles, Life Cycles, Culture Cycles, and Living Cycles as "the cross sectional view of Japanese society,' which gives a 'more accurate picture of the seemingly disparate realities of Japanese architecture today (p2).' Igarashi provides a more profession-focussed view of this phenomenon by recalling the 1995 earthquake that hit Kobe, which undermined the Deconstructivist 'tremor-as-metaphor designs,' supported 'simple, transparent Modernism,' as well as highlighted the need for reconstruction (p3). Finding fewer jobs, the 'post-bubble' architects like Atelier Bow-Wow and Mikan consolidated their efforts into collectives which undertook renovations, extensions, and events and exhibitions, thereby expanding the disciplinary field (p3).

The four themes of *Parallel Nippon* consist of projects loosely bound in pairs acting as 'parallel' responses. Urban Cycles features distinctive minor sub-themes of Egg Grid System, Open Working System, Hot Spring Economy, Skin in Landscape, Glass and Geometry, Refurbishing and Redress, Office Tower, Verticality and Horizontality, Conversion, Abandoned Schools and Factories. It focuses on 'small decentralised cities' and the declining emphasis on 'national projects by big government,' giving way to 'small government' driven initiatives (Japan Foundation, 2013, p4). In Life Cycles we find Kindergarten, Communal Life for Self Reliance, Elementary Schools in Urban Development, School in Gulf/School in Himalaya, Big Roof, Expression by Concrete/Expression by Timber, Roof Terrace, Hanging Terrace, Regular/ Irregular, Steps to Another World, Houses for Aging Society, Landscape for Death, Symbolism of Lights, Simple/ Chaotic, Hiroshima/Nagasaki. It focuses on the design of public facilities that have 'come to reflect user affiliations and backgrounds,' provision of handicap accessibility, and the emergence multifunctional buildings that house schools, housing for the elderly as well as disaster-relief shelters when needed, reflecting ageing society, and a reduction in birth rate (Japan Foundation, 2013, p 6–7). Culture Cycles and Living Cycles are similarly curated. They respectively focus on the new role of cultural industries in regional growth, and the convention of standardized housing competing with convivial affluent living tendencies apparent in the return to the traditional Japanese style quarters.

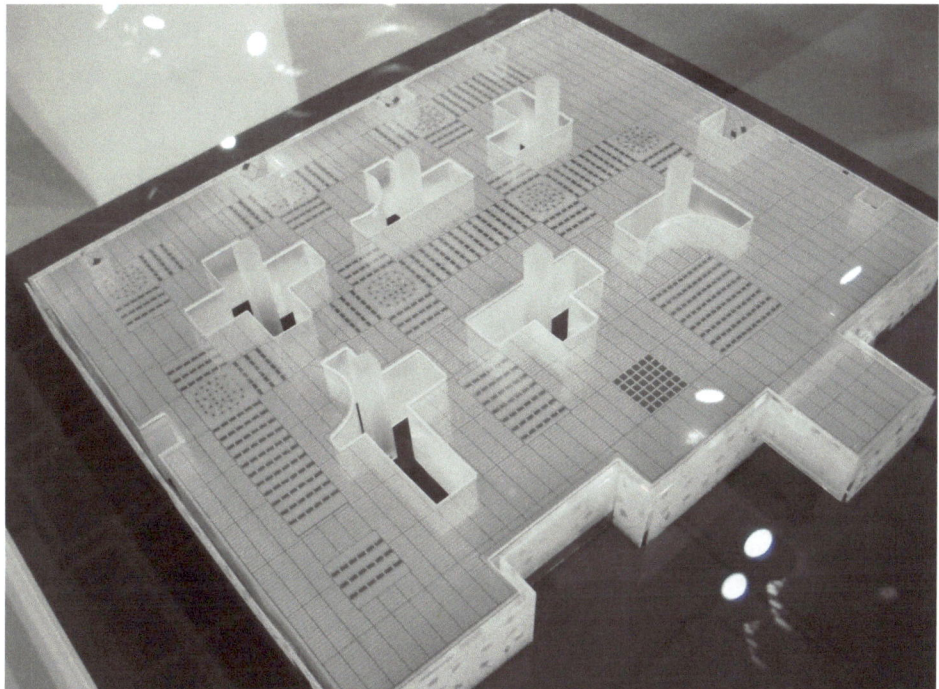

Figure 8 Parallel Nippon [Photo: Anuradha Chatterjee]

The width and depth of *Parallel Nippon* is a force to reckon with. It is not merely a historical but also a critical survey of the current state of the discipline. Curated and installed with great beauty and elegance in a somewhat compromising gallery of the Japan Foundation inside Chifley Square, it presents a fresh perspective on architectural historiography as well as exhibitions. It does so by using the curatorial lens of the four themes. This allows the discussion to progress beyond categorizing works in a chronological, regional, and typological manner. It also takes the focus off the tools of architectural history—time, place, and object—placing it instead within a wider economic, social, and cultural history of the Japan. Fittingly, then the focus is on ways of life and values, invented and reinvented within the broader context of tradition, modernity, and the contemporary. The use of major themes with distinctive minor sub-themes provides an effective way to cut through disciplinary boundaries of architecture, construction, planning, and urban design as well as architectural typologies of housing, factories, institutional and educational buildings, places of worship, and museums and galleries.

1.6 Urban Resonances: Two Exhibitions at Customs House Sydney

Customs House, Sydney, showcased two resonant exhibitions—the travelling exhibition titled *People Building Better Cities: Participation and Inclusive Urbanization* by Global Studio (under Anna Rubbo), and a more locally produced (City of Sydney) and viewed exhibit titled the *Next Stop: 21st Century George Street*. This is an interesting and timely turn of events, given Customs House's long-standing role in showcasing innovative practices in digital architecture, 3D visualization, and lighting technologies. Architectural agendas are not timeless. From situated modernisms, to eco-tech approaches to sustainability, to digital and media environments, and urbanism and city making, architecture's reshaping is constant. The 21st century agenda is the recasting of architecture to architecture + urbanism. The framings are multiple—sustainability, inadequate infrastructure, public participation, and agency, and lack of democratized public domains. Neither is urbanism new nor is architecture ignorant of it, yet there is a need to reiterate this duality. Nevertheless, urbanism at least in Australia is marked by the shift from delivery to agency. This is less about design and more about designing in social sustainability, as participation and dialogue emphasizes ownership of solutions as arrived at collaboratively rather than those that are imposed. The two exhibitions in Customs House bear out this tendency.

Led by Professor Anna Rubbo, *People Building Better Cities* is a joint project of Global Studio and Columbia University's Center for Sustainable Urban Development, and has been made possible by the SAPPI Ideas That Matter grant. The exhibition would have visited ten countries, including China, India, Philippines, South Africa, and the United States, having already been to Thailand in February and Brazil (Rio de Janeiro) in March 2013. The motto of *People Building Better Cities* is as follows: 'Resilient, sustainable, equitable, and inclusive cities must involve people as partners.' They explain that inclusive urbanization can occur only 'through innovations in participatory design and planning (Rubbo, 2013).' While the exhibition's focus is on developing countries, it speaks to urban issues in developed countries such as growing inequality and climate change, foregrounding the merits of collaborative decision making and planning. These were borne out in the panel discussion titled *Citizens and City Making*, which questions surrounding rights to the city as the NSW government seeks to make planning reforms and workshop titled *Public Engagement in City Design and Planning: Barriers, Opportunities and Ideas Workshop* that sought to explore, document, and provide directions for Australian urbanists and planners.

Figure 9 People Building Better Cities [Photo: Peter Murphy]

People Building Better Cities builds on the contributions of the Global Studio, in which students, academics, and professionals collaborate to undertake 'community-based action and research' projects with the 'aim of helping to improve people's lives in disadvantaged communities (Rubbo et al., 2014).' To date some 500 people from over 30 countries, over 66 universities and 11 disciplines have participated in its activities in Istanbul in 2005; Vancouver in 2006; and in Johannesburg in 2007, 2008, 2009 (Rubbo et al., 2014).' While Global Studios projects in 2012 in Bhopal like *Kabadkhana, Just Communication, and Inclusive City Centre* gain potency and authenticity from being rooted in real communities with real needs, the translation, extension, and interpretation into Australian planning debates seems strangely out of place and elusive.

Next Stop: 21st Century George Street showcase the City of Sydney's Draft George Street Concept Design for public feedback is available at http://sydneyyoursay.com.au/georgestreet (City of Sydney, 2013a). The proposal is a response to the New South Wales government's proposed mass transport light rail, which aims to pedestrianize some parts of George Street, connect Randwick in the east to Dulwich Hill in the west, and to key transport interchanges (Central Station and Circular Quay), and above all 'transform George Street into a *world class main street* with light rail for business, tourism, and street life (City of Sydney, 2013b).' The proposal sheds light on the City's direction in terms of 'types and configuration of street trees, paving, public art, public domain furniture, lighting, and signage (City of Sydney, 2013b).' The exhibition *Next Stop* consists of two sectional models of the George Street precinct, cards on which people can submit their views, a website that invites electronic submissions, and laser cut props that announce: 'There are presently only six public benches along the length of George Street;' 'There are presently only 12 outdoor dining licenses along the length of George Street;' and 'Over two hundred new trees representing a five-fold increase in the canopy along George Street.'

Figure 10 Next Stop: 21st Century George Street [Photo: Peter Murphy]

The draft report identifies eight key elements of design—The Light Rail, Light Rail Stops, Paving, Trees, Furniture, Lighting, Art, and The Edges—that are layered as well as integrated. The design approach is one of visual minimalism, such that the above-listed elements of design are unobtrusive to the extent of disappearance. This is not necessarily bad, except that this does not automatically support the claims about comfort and vitality. The minimalist approach to design is informed solely by physical study of built environments, and conclusions that derive from simple deductions about traffic and vitality of streets. City of Sydney locates George Street as the future street in the chronology of European and North American streets like the Champs Élysées, La Rambla, Strøget, Copenhagen, Swanston Street, Melbourne, and Sections of Broadway (including Times Square), New York (City of Sydney, 2013c). This is done without really acknowledging that history, sense of place, vitality, and public engagement cannot be manufactured, but enabled and witnessed.

The two exhibitions are a contrast. *People Building Better Cities* explores real communities with real needs, doing more with less, and generating resources and income. In contrast, *Next Stop* showcases a gift, a project valued at $180 million. The modes of participation are as different as the lessons in urbanism. While People *Building Better Cities* explores and locates urban issues of infrastructure, health, and well-being, Next Stop takes this as a given, as an entitlement, and seeks no further opportunity for enhancement. Participation as presence, effort, and collaboration in *People Building Better Cities* is shifted and made somewhat remote in the *Next Stop*, as participation is by the virtual, anonymous, and disembodied citizen. From *having a stake*, participation is transformed into having a say. Nevertheless, both exhibitions firmly highlight a shift. Occupation of public space is not just physical. It is about occupying the public domain of ideas, information, and above all, knowledge.

1.7　Living in the Ruins

One of the most unusual exhibitions to open in Sydney was *Living in the Ruins* in the UTS Gallery. The exhibition is curated by Adam Jasper and Holly Williams in association with New York based magazine, *Cabinet,* and it aims to present the history of 20th century as one of 'false starts, obsolete technologies, and unrealized utopias (Williams and Jasper 2013).' The curators note that the exhibition is an 'archaeological dig into the material culture that shapes our present.' It draws together 'objects from art, science, and ethnography in an investigation of the ruins, remnants, and ill-fated prototypes that defined a century already far enough in the past to be foreign to us, but close enough that we still have no fitting monuments for it (Williams and Jasper, 2013).' The most obvious metaphor is the Wunderkammer or a cabinet of curiosities that 'traverses diverse themes from islands to explosions and giant spheres.' *Living in the Ruins* is a combination of artefacts from the 'the Macleay Museum and the University of Sydney, the Museum of Old and New Art, the Westpac Archives and the Powerhouse Museum with articles from Cabinet and works by Australian and international artists including Daniel Knorr, Patrick Pound, Gianni Motti, Hany Armanious, Maria Friberg, Roman Signer, Sarah Pickering, Nicholas Mangan, Tracey Moffatt, David Haines & Joyce Hinterding, Vicky Browne, the Institute of Critical Zoologists, Michael Stevenson, Jaki Middleton & David Lawrey, Nadia Wagner, Alex Gawronski, Lillian O'Neil, Matthew Shannon, Koji Ryui and others (Williams and Jasper, 2013).' A more complete archive and description of the objects are available at http://livingintheruins.net/, which will remain active for a period of time.

Williams notes that the exhibition is designed to evoke a fluid entry and circulation. It was arranged by theme, but a more hands-on approach to curation, display, and installation meant that the process was iterative, and hence not a didactic outcome of themes or rooms (Williams, 2013). Of course, resonances between object and space (and across spaces) in terms of material, size, texture, and volume was important. Williams' insights into the process of curation are not mundane. They disclose a non-linear creative act of thinking and doing, merging evidence and intuition, such that the final exhibit is not a mere translation/execution of the curatorial plan. These insights also suggest a hybrid—the bodies of the curator(s) and his/her objects—collapsing subject and object—such that they are co-informed. The overt curatorial stance of archaeology is distinct from a historical perspective in its attachment to material objects and fictions. Williams notes that the reason for focusing on the 20th century is that it does not have a clear narrative and it is close yet remote to warrant a revisit (Williams, 2013). Perhaps, Williams is alluding to a 20th-century uncanny, where the familiar and unfamiliar, and the adjacent and the distant coalesce and collapse into each other.

Figure 11 Installation View, Room 1B, Living in the Ruins [Photo: Alex Davies]

The exhibition is informed by the premise of the magazine:

By operating with the most expansive and inclusive definition of 'culture' possible, one that includes both the quotidian and the extraordinary, Cabinet aims to foster curiosity about the world we have made and inhabit. We believe that curiosity is the very basis of ethics insofar as a deeper understanding of our social and material cultures encourages us both to be better custodians of the world and at the same time allows us to imagine it otherwise (Cabinet, 2012a).

Living in the Ruins is therefore a spatial/visual translation of the text/publication-based Cabinet. In other words, issues of publication, text, image, editing, and printing is then taken to a three-dimensional level of exhibition, object, collation, curation, spatial resonances, and display. The Reading Room is hence simultaneously literal and metaphorical. It is a display and a place where back issues of *Cabinet* can be browsed through—a fantastical coming together of text and image, real and the irreal. The metaphorical exchange between the exhibition and the magazine is progressed as the rooms are also thought of as chapters, suggesting that these not only stand-alone but that resonances and re-visitations are expected.

Williams points to another important curatorial stance, which is the role of curiosity is also to unsettle perceptual habits. Hence, a very obvious aspect of the exhibition (and perhaps frustrating for some) is that there are no labels. Whilst this can be considered elitist, it is also a productive frustration that is prompted by Michel Foucault's emphasis on curiosity. Cabinet cites Foucault's statement from *The Masked Philosopher:* 'I dream of a new age of curiosity.' He defined it as that which

Figure 12 Installation View, Room 1F, Living in the Ruins [Photo: Alex Davies]

suggests something altogether different: it evokes "concern"; it evokes the care one takes for what exists and could exist; a readiness to find strange and singular what surrounds us; a certain relentlessness to break up our familiarities and to regard otherwise the same things; a fervor to grasp what is happening and what passes; a casualness in regard to the traditional hierarchies of the important and the essential Cabinet (2012b).

In *Living in the Ruins,* the visitor realizes within five minutes that the expectation to be lead through the exhibits through labels that connect to a catalogue is thwarted. Indeed it is like a/the *Cabinet* (of curiosity), where labels are not needed or desired. Whilst this move is contemporaneous with immersive design of recent galleries and museums, it is not formally contrived. Williams connects this also to spiritual practices in Zen Buddhism, involving the forsaking of the ego) as the absence of labels encourages the visitor to let go of known (hence safe) ways of navigating the terrain of exhibits. The perceptual habits are shifted by combining museological display style with contemporary art practice. The visitor explores through a mixture of orientation and disorientation. It is in fact an embodied process as the visitor 'finds' themselves in finding the object in the room. Williams acknowledges Museum of Old and New Art in Tasmania (MONA) as a contemporary, with Cabinet magazine predating the conception of MONA (Williams, 2013).

Figure 13 Fabacus 1964 (First Australian Bank's Accounting Computer Used in Sydney) computer panel, installed in Sydney, manufactured by General Electric, 61 × 72.5 × 13.5 cm, on loan from The Westpac Banking Group Archives [Photo: Alex Davies]

The importance of this exhibition is that it challenges the sanitized quality of architecture exhibitions seen in Sydney. Architectural design and practice as education and professional practice is messy. Yes, architecture must always conceal its detritus and prehistory to present itself as forever and always new. This is evidenced in exhibitions that almost always consist of posters and panels with models as a format, filing away the untranslatable, failed concepts, lost ideas, representational incompletions, and conceptual revisitations, all of which form the instruments and technologies of architecture. *Living in the Ruin,* hence, is a possibility of rethinking the future of architecture exhibitions as material, technological, and hence cultural histories of the practice.

References

Australian Institute of Landscape Architects (2012), Sydney from All Angles. Available from: http://www.sydneyallangles.org.au/ [Accessed 29 April 2014].

Cabinet (2012a), About Us. Available from: cabinetmagazine.org/information/about [Accessed 29 April 2014].

Cabinet (2012b), A succinct statement on curiosity by Michel Foucault that sums up Cabinet's mission better than we can. Available from: http://www.cabinetmagazine.org/information/foucault.php [Accessed 29 April 2014].

Cameron M (2010), 'Examining the Connections between Architecture and Jewellery,' in *Craft Australia Library Series: Conference Presentations.* Available from: www.craftaustralia.org.au/library/presentation.php?id=jewellery_and_architecture [Accessed 29 April 2014].

City of Sydney (2013a), *Transforming George Street.* Available from: http://sydneyyoursay.com.au/georgestreet [Accessed 29 April 2014].

City of Sydney (2013b), *Factsheet: George Street Concept Design.* Available from: http://sydneyyoursay.com.au/georgestreet/documents/12135/download [Accessed 29 April 2014].

City of Sydney (2013c), *George Street Concept Design,* Available from http://sydneyyoursay.com.au/georgestreet/documents/ 12155/download [Accessed 29 April 2014].

Decker U (2012), *Press Release.* Available from: http://www.utedecker.com/jewellery/ute_decker_architectural_jewellery_LFA2012.pdf [Accessed 29 April 2014].

Furuto A (2013), 'Parallel Nippon: Contemporary Japanese Architecture 1996-2006,' *ArchDaily.* Available from: http://www.archdaily.com/?p=346806 [Accessed 17 Apr 2014].

Hauesler HM (2014), 'Hypersurface Architecture [Redux],' in Chatterjee A, *Surface and Deep Histories: Critiques, and Practices in Art, Architecture, and Design,* Cambridge Scholarly Publishing, UK, 69-86.

HK+NP Studio, Profile. Available from: https://www.linkedin.com/company/hk-np-studio. [Accessed 29 April 2014].

Japan Foundation (2013), *Parallel Nippon: Contemporary Japanese Architecture 1996-2006* [Catalogue of an Exhibition at Japan Foundation Gallery, Sydney] Sydney: Japan Foundation.

Ripoll M (2012), Interview.

Rubbo A (2013), *People Building Better Cities: Participation and Inclusive Urbanization.* Available from: http://peoplebuildingbettercities.org/about/ [Accessed 17 Apr 2014].

Rubbo A, Sclar E, Garau P, and Carolini G, *Global Studio.* Available from: http://theglobalstudio.com/category/about/[Accessed 29 April 2014].

UTS. Open Agenda Competition. Available from: www.utsarchitecture.net/openagenda/[Accessed 29 April 2014]. Williams H (2013), Interview, 13 May 2013

Williams H and Jasper A (2013), *Living in the Ruins.* Available from: http://livingintheruins.net/ [Accessed 29 April 2014].

Chapter 02

Talking Point

Abstract: *Talking Point* presents a range of talks that were held at the Surry Hills Library (City of Sydney), University of New South Wales (Utzon Lecture Series), Historic Houses Trust, Museum of Contemporary Arts, City Recital Hall organized by NSW Planning & Infrastructure, and TED talks. Public lectures and talks are part of any institution in the city such as a museum or a gallery or an architecture school. Above all it is a form of media or mass communication. Positioned with a city, these lectures are not merely entertaining, informative, and educational, but they are also a crucial part of democracy and citizenship.

Key words: Sustainability, domesticity, criticism, density, infrastructure

2.1 Introduction

Talking Point presents a range of talks that were held at the Surry Hills Library (City of Sydney), University of New South Wales (Utzon Lecture Series), Historic Houses Trust, Museum of Contemporary Arts, City Recital Hall organized by NSW Planning & Infrastructure, and TED talks. Of course other talks of significance also happen regularly at or organized by Australian Institute of Architects at Tusculum, University of Sydney, and University of Technology, Make Space for Architecture, Architectural Association of Australia, Design Centre, and other community libraries, with a range of talks organized in various locations during the Sydney Architecture Festival and the Design Week. This chapter covers only a small range of talks. Talks not covered here include the Alexandra Lange symposium (because it has been extensively reported already). The talks focus not only on practical concerns like urbanization, housing density, infrastructure planning but also on theoretical issues like criticism and spatial intelligence.

Public lectures and talks are part of any institution in the city such as a museum or a gallery or an architecture school. Above all it is a form of media or mass communication. Positioned with a city, these lectures are not merely entertaining, informative, and educational, but they are also a crucial part of enabling democracy and citizenship. Historically, people become citizens by being part of debates that shape society. If knowledge is power, then the public lectures and talks are a partial and conditional sharing of this power by addressing an audience of 'non-experts.' Of course, public lectures are also modes through which ideas developed internally in an institution are communicated to the society at large with the hope of gaining legitimacy and sustained relevance. In contemporary society, public lectures and talks also serve as an implicit index of the intellectual well-being of a society or an institution. It is also a sign of intellectual progress, where interest in experience and ideas is valued over the consumption of commodities alone. These are open lectures, but one has to know that open does not mean really open as intangible barriers of knowledge, association, subscription, and so on, do in fact cast doubt over the publicness of these public lectures.

Small Spaces/Big Ideas highlights the obsession with largeness (in domestic dwellings in Australia and Sydney), showcasing the design of smaller dwellings, equally rich with numerous spatial possibilities and experiences, suggesting that bigger is not always better. *Talking House* considers the different typologies of domestic architecture through history as well as the persistence of these typologies in building practice, shedding light on what works and what does not. Michael Newman's talk *Form follows Flow* demonstrates that the meaning of sustainability is not achievable by focusing on individual components of urban life and their form alone but by thinking of them as an interconnected thermodynamic system comprising of flows. *Talking Up the City* pursues the idea of sustainability, as Ed Glaeser (author of *Triumph of the City: How Our Greatest Invention Makes Us Richer, Smarter, Greener, Healthier and Happier*, Penguin) argues that the sustainability of a city, especially a financial one, is dependent solely and mostly upon density.

However, *Spatial Intelligence and New Domesticities* shows that according to urbanists like Tarsha Finney from UTS and AA, density is not enough for achieving sustainable cities: we need to re-think and expand conventional definitions of domesticity. Gerard Reinmuth and Anthony Burke, also from UTS, argue that the identity of the architect should be redefined to include her/him in the network of actors, in addition to drawing upon the spatial thinking and intelligence ingrained in every human being in the planning of our built environments. And finally, *Building Sites* presents the idea of 'infrastructural topography' or 'inhabited topography' developed by New York architectural firm Weiss and Manfredi. This multidisciplinary approach integrates architecture, infrastructure, and landscape, such that planning of denser and more sustainable cities can be done in more integrated ways.

2.2   Small Spaces, Big Ideas

On 28 April 2012, a quiet Saturday afternoon in the Surry Hills Library, inner city Sydney, is vitalized by the talk *Small Spaces, Big Ideas,* delivered by architects Christopher Polly and Sam Crawford, and organized by the City of Sydney Council and presented with the Australian Institute of Architects (represented by Andrew Burns). The premise of the talk as noted by the City of Sydney is: 'In a period of diminishing land availability, living small becomes a necessary and logical way of life (City of Sydney, 2012a).' The talk is also pertinent for other reasons and trends such as the move towards designing and delivering compact cities in Australia; reducing the ecological footprint; domestic downsizing by empty-nester Australians; and the demand for affordable (and rental) housing for a wider demographic in Sydney.

A lack of housing supply compounded by escalating real estate prices has been a growing concern not only for home buyers but also for state and local government agencies, urban planners, and architects. Noting that 'not everyone wants a large and elaborate house,' New South Wales Department of Infrastructure and Planning Minister Brad Hazzard was instrumental in ensuring the move towards smaller houses on smaller lots of land (Hazzard, 2012). While the average lot size for individual houses in Sydney has been between 450 sq m and 750 sq m, there has been a steady and increasing demand for lots as small as 150 sq m (Ooi, 2011; Crawford, 2012). This has been accompanied by a move away from larger stand-alone houses and a return to semi-detached and terrace (or row) style of housing—a housing option often chosen by empty nesters wanting to downsize, and first homebuyers who need affordable homes (Hazzard, 2013). The talk by Christopher Polly and Sam Crawford reflected this trend.

Sam Crawford noted that Australia has largest house size in the world (243 sq m, a figure sourced from Simon Johanson's article in Sydney Morning Herald (2011). Crawford mentioned examples of people experimenting with reducing house sizes in the United States, Denmark, and Japan, to foreground the key distinction between expectation and need. Using examples of his own projects, he demonstrated that more space could be achieved on small lots and within older existing houses, like his own house built within the existing shell of a Queen Anne style standalone house.

The key design principles of this approach were identified as spilt levels to create different spaces creating the feeling of more space; the use of different materials to create the effect of spaciousness; designing multi-functional spaces like the staircase landing at ground level that is extended into a seating space, or the low window sill of a large south facing window used as a kids play area, or the integration of bookshelves and storage spaces along staircase walls. It was also noted that the smallness of the house demands a careful consideration of acoustical buffers.

Christopher Polly discussed Elliott Ripper House (161 sq m), Haines House (115 sq m), and Darling Point Penthouse (100 sq m)—all small dwellings, which explore design strategies like the use of elements stretching across one space to another; creating adaptable spaces, through the use of internal building elements such as folding metal panels that can be folded back or folded out to increase or decrease room sizes. Central to creating the impression of space was light, both artificial and natural. Polly noted that this was achieved through a choreographed arrangement of strip windows on the exterior wall and on the internal walls to allow light to flow between rooms—an experience further augmented through the use of reflective white surfaces.

A short and an interesting talk was attended by built environment enthusiasts, most of them not even architects, and complemented by the presenters' enthusiasm in responding to lay queries as well as more searching, discipline specific questions. This, I think, was a very positive outcome of the profession's recent consciousness of communicating ethical and urban concerns informing practice to seek and sustain legitimacy and meaningfulness of architectural practice against the needs and expectations of multiple stakeholders in the built environment. Since the talk, there have been recent developments on part of the NSW Department of Infrastructure and Planning which seek to enable changes in planning rules and practices such that lots as small as 125 sq m are allowed in areas which can support high densities; and townhouses, terrace houses, and studio dwellings are encouraged so as to provide a diversity and affordability of housing options, which will cater to the needs of Sydney's growing population.

2.3 'Form follows Flow'

Michael Neuman (Professor of Sustainable Urbanism, newly appointed at the Built Environment, University of New South Wales) delivered the Fifth Annual Paul Reid Lecture in Urban Design: 'Sticks and Stones will Make My Bones: Durability in Design. The lecture set out to interrogate the following questions: 'How do we know when a city is truly sustainable? Is it even possible for cities in a global age to be so? How can professional practices retool to be sustainable urbanisms? Urbanists design forms, traditionally. Yet in nature as in cities, humans, other species, and ecosystems live, evolve, and adapt through processes (Neuman, 2012a).' There were three aspects to the lecture: (a) material sustainability; (b) sustainability as similar to the thermodynamic system; and (c) the city as a sustainable system.

Neuman explains that 'sticks and stones' are the natural materiality developed over time; 'make' is what designers create and produce; and 'bones' are the infrastructure that supports everyday life—ideally synthesized into one. Durability is connected to sustainability principles such as resilience and flexibility. Hence, using natural materials like wood, bamboo, iron, steel is sensible, because these materials can be reprocessed; have a low life cycle cost; acquire other qualities over time; and are resistant to heating and cooling as they have evolved from nature. Using the image of a cliff face, Neuman argues: 'Form is understood as the interaction between nature and culture. In nature, processes convert flows to form, and in culture, processes convert materials into meaning (Neuman, 2012b).'

Neuman then goes onto explain sustainability through the laws of thermodynamics. He argues that urban practice and theory is spatial only and it does not engage time. While it does engage the theory of thermodynamics, it does only partially. It thinks only of conserving energy and matter, entirely bypassing the concept of entropy (irreversible dissipation and decay of matter and energy over time). Hence, the inability to grasp the constant input that cities need to maintain life, proportional to the size and complexity of the city. Neuman advances a (new) view of sustainability based on flows—natural, topographical, human, digital, information, financial, and so on. Flow and form are in a constant bi-directional or reciprocal relation, evident in the manner in which nature sustains itself. Neuman states: 'Flow determines form. Form follows flow (Neuman, 2012b).' He suggests that by using the thermodynamic concept of entropy and rate process theory, sustainability can be mapped using a formula such that it is a measurable and objective practice.

Neuman then uses the analogy of the tree to explain sustainable urbanism, which is when cities are understood as systems. The tree is regarded as the paragon of 'permanence and continuity,' as the archetype of the web of life. Neuman suggests that trees are 'open systems connected to other open systems,' complex yet resilient, a repository of knowledge and intelligence. 'Sustainable urbanism is networked urbanism,' argues Neuman, because they are open and interconnected networks of processes and not just forms (Neuman, 2012b).

The lecture present ideas that are innovative, complex for the right reasons, applicable to a range of scales, from the material choice to infrastructure. It is objective at the same time aspires better design and planning practices. Rod Simpson's closing of the lecture brings out the idealities in Neuman's propositions against the conservative business models in current practice, which disallows quick or palpable change. Simpson also suggests that facts generated by formulas can gain agency only through informed political processes, activism, community engagement, and communication, and that it is only through these complementary processes that sustainable urbanism can even begin to become a reality.

2.4   Talking House

The theme of the dwelling is quite fittingly explored by the Historic Houses Trust, Sydney in the 'Sydney Open Talks: House,' that ran from Thursdays 26 April to14 June 2012. Historically, housing has functioned as the key cultural symbol as well as instrument of colonization, ownership, commodity, belonging, citizenship, and more recently sustainability and compact urbanism. The talk series covers eight typologies—Bungalow, Apartment, Villa, Mansion, Shack, Terrace, Project Home, and Portable Home—covering varied cultural, economic, climatic, and ecological milieus in Sydney, NSW, and Australia (Historic Houses Trust, 2012a).

Dr James Broadbent considers the mythologies surrounding the bungalow whereas Scott Robertson maps the rise and fall of the Bungalow from its introduction in 1906 to its decline in the 1930s. Dr Caroline Butler-Bowdon considers the tower, the slab, and the walk-up Apartment types in Sydney with Adam Haddow reflecting on the challenges as well as the rewards for creating 'new living environments' that foster compact living in cities. While Scott Carlin locates Sydney's inheritance of the British suburban Villa as the origin of the 'love of the quarter acre block and Sydney's urban sprawl,' Philip Goad uncovers the two kinds of Villas, based on conceptions of the landscape as pastoral and wilderness, arguing that the Villa is a 'resilient and romantic ideal (Historic Houses Trust, 2012b).' The Mansion is considered historically by Charles Pickett, who observes the 'Australian desire to dwell in excess,' from colonial to contemporary times. This is complemented by Jonathan Chancellor's presentation, which notes that the 'residential monumentalism' of McMansions has failed to gain cultural legitimacy (Historic Houses Trust, 2012b).

The Shack is presented as domestic architecture without architects by Michael Bogle, complemented by Peter Stutchbury's discussion that regards the shack as the logical response to coastal occupation and economy in Australia. The Terrace, according to Keri Huxley, has changed from its humble beginnings as working class dwellings in the nineteenth century to gentrified commodities in the contemporary Sydney (Historic Houses Trust, 2012b). This is complemented by Hannah Tribe's presentation of a Victorian, a Federation, and a Georgian terrace, which demonstrates the individualization of typologies that appear to have a uniform exterior form. The link between successful Project Homes and the involvement of architects and designers with project builders is considered by Dr Judith O'Callaghan (Historic Houses Trust, 2012b). This is accompanied by Tone Wheeler's discussion of Environa Studio's Project Homes that seek the middle path of negotiating standardized design of the draftsman and the customized design of the architect. The Portable House according to Megan Martin is an outcome of intersecting political, cultural, and economic factors, like the colonial expansion, military endeavour, and gold discovery. Sean Godsell imparts political potency to this typology, as projects such as the Bus Shelter House, Park Bench House, and Picnic Table House respond to the urban infrastructure's resistance to occupation by homeless citizens (Historic Houses Trust, 2012b).

Presented as eight conversations between historians, writers, and commentators on the one hand, and architects, policy makers, and property specialists on the other, the talks close the supposed gap between theory and history, and the practice and the contemporary, as well as that between the ordinary and the innovative. Even though the talks do not overtly engage social and cultural practices of domesticity (based on ethnicity, gender, and class) focusing exclusively on the object, the dwelling, they generate a great deal of optimism by showcasing the breadth and depth of scholarship and expertise that exists on Housing in Sydney.

2.5 Culture of Criticism

Figure 14 Mordant Wing, Museum of Contemporary Art, Sydney [Photo: Anuradha Chatterjee]

The opening of Museum of Contemporary Art Australia (MCA) annexe by architect Sam Marshall on the 29 March 2012 was met with intense debate and discussion. These debates were tabled in a public forum, *Open Conversation,* held on the 03 May 2012 by Make-Space for Architecture (MS4A), an independent agency that 'seeks to challenge and recalibrate normative ideologies found in architecture, design and the built environment of Sydney (MS4A, 2014).' Held at the School of Architecture, University of Technology Sydney (UTS), and moderated by John de Manincor (UTS and DRAW, an architectural firm), Open Conversation included the following panellists: Sam Marshall, Architect; Andrew Donaldson, Architect; Paul Berkemeier, Architect; Philip Cox (AO), Cox Architecture; Elizabeth Farrelly, Opinion Writer for *Sydney Morning Herald* (SMH); and Imogene Tudor, Director, MS4A. The conversations are prompted by Farelley's note on the lack of spatial delight and clarity of circulation in MCA (Farrelly, 2012); Andrew Anderson's observation that the building lacks nuanced and shifting visual qualities; and Philip Cox's declaration that the building appears to be championing the 'bland architecture of old with bland architecture of new (Aston, 2012).' They also probe additional issues of the architectural brief, the white box interior, and the elusive big idea.

MCA, however, demands and deserves a slower meander. It delivers the following: a strong and seamless connection from the foreshore to the street; a tortured but fascinating sightline from the entrance through to the foyer to the gallery space on Level 2; beautifully crafted staircases that provide a view of the sandstone walls of the original building; the transparent lift shafts that allow episodic but dramatic views out to the harbour; the plasterboard interior lining which transforms artificial light into a luminous glow that encounters the daylight filtering into the building. The restrained palette can be interpreted through the metaphysical lenses of absence and light—approaches that underpin minimalist approaches and that address the issue of spatial delight in a manner that is not immediately graspable.

Figure 15 Mordant Wing, MCA, Foyer Level 1, Looking out towards Circular Quay [Photo: Anuradha Chatterjee]

The intriguing thing about Open Conversation, however, is not the substance of the conversation, but the manner in which it happens. It was bookended by published articles that closely followed each other. These include two articles in *Sydney Morning Herald* in March 2012: Heath Aston's MCA's Chequered Reception (04 March) and Elizabeth Farrelly's Spatial Delight Gets Lost at MCA (27 March); followed closely by three articles in Australian Design Review in May 2012: David Neustein's MCA: Open Conversation or Guarded Debate? (04 May), Gerard Reinmuth's Critical Thinking (07 May), and Gillian Serisier's Lines of Division: The New MCA in Sydney (09 May). These articles are closely followed by Farrelly's Bold, Frank Criticism Can Only Nourish Architecture (10 May) in *Sydney Morning Herald*. While Neustein (2012) vividly narrates the event, portraying the multiple tones and voices that speak differently and discordantly about MCA, Reinmuth (2012) questions the manner of critique undertaken by and through this event and the missed opportunities. And while Seisier (2012) restores the MCA to its rightful glory by providing a fuller understanding of the exhibition spaces, Farelley (2012b) recounts the Open Conversation, continuing to defend the critic's privilege to opinions that must be fearlessly expressed.

Notwithstanding these contributions, the *Open Conversation* is firstly (and mostly) theatrical. Its boundaries held tightly together (hosted, moderated, and published), and complemented by conversations between the various participants (at the table, and off the table through blogs and social media), the *Open Conversation* calls upon the act of witnessing the occurrence of debate. Secondly, the urgency to settle the meaning of the building counteracts the expectation that proper critique ought to be a sustained activity. It should be capable of maintaining interest as well as energy, without simply providing material for instant consumption. Thirdly, the *Open Conversation* was shaped by very precise inter- and intra-professional associations and institutional settings. It is but one of the many critical networks existing in Sydney. And finally, even though the debates were undertaken in a public forum, they should not be mistaken as representative of public perspective on the building, as they did not include artists, art critics or writers, curators, visitors, staff, and guides, despite the insistence that the speaking voice of the public is the foundation of good criticism. One can ask how open was the *Open Conversation*? In doing so, it opens up questions about the future and form of architectural criticism in Australia.

2.6   Talking (up) the City

The culture of debate emerging strongly in Sydney informed the free community discussion held on the 20 June at the City Recital Hall. The title of the talk was Urban Conversations: *Triumph of the City*. It was a three-part event, with the highlight being the talk by guest speaker from Harvard University Professor Edward Glaeser who discussed the arguments contained in his book Triumph of the City. This was followed by panel discussion and questions from the audience. The panel consisted of New South Wales Government Architect Peter Poulet, and the Department of Planning & Infrastructure's Giovanni Cirillo (now Director, Planning Lab) and

Norma Shankie-Williams (now technical director at AECOM), and Sarah Hill, President, Planning Institute of Australia NSW Division (current President is David Ryan), mediated by Australian Broadcasting Corporations' James O'Loghlin. The event is underpinned by the premise that Sydney's 4.2 million population is expected to rise to more than 5.6 million by 2031, which will necessitate creative thinking around the provision of social, cultural, physical and economic infrastructure.

Figure 16 Urban Conversations Talk, Professor Edward Glaeser, Image courtesy NSW Department of Planning & Infrastructure, [Photo: Paul Wright]

Through a historical survey of American cities in the 20th century, Glaeser explains that infrastructure needs are crucial because every historical city was linked to ports, harbours, waterway, railways, and roads. Glaeser argues the following: Cities are humanity's greatest invention; density is related to income productivity; density fosters proximity, and adjacency which in turn makes possible the collaborative knowledge economy; knowledge economy is the basis of wealth and prosperity; and increasing wealth of cities prompts the questioning of liveability and the benchmarking of liveable cities. Glaeser notes that cities support entrepreneurship and diminish unemployment, providing an antidote to financial crisis (historically and currently) but failure of infrastructure is also what makes cities fail. His talk is interesting because it not only talks up the city, but it also demonstrates the city as simultaneously being the site of failures and successes.

The key topics and instances of city making in the panel discussion included urban renewal at Green Square, as providing jobs and amenities, and the Eastern Distributor as having re-energized Surry Hills (Cirillo); Revitalization of Darling Harbour (Poulet); Developing Penrith, Parramatta, and Liverpool as mature regional cities distinct from the city along the Harbour (Williams); Need for leadership in city making and emphasizing the idea of active places and spaces in the city as creating a market to invest in (Hill); Systemic thinking and future planning to design sustainable cities (Glaeser); Engaging the voice of the community for successful urban renewal (Williams); and Greening cities to reduce the heat island effect, increase well-being, and tackle urban food production (Poulet). The panel discussion was a bit haphazard. But, it was inspiring to see the panel members place emphasis on newness and optimism, and open channels of communication as the fundamentals to addressing urban challenges. The questions from the audience were many and pertinent, with one member in particular questioning the relationship between erosion of psychological well-being and cities. Glaeser responded by citing the frequency of youth suicides in country towns as a counterpoint.

Figure 17 Urban Conversations Panel, Image courtesy NSW Department of Planning & Infrastructure [Photo: Paul Wright]

What was slightly disappointing was the American voice to Australian issues. Whilst Glaeser's talk was insightful, a complementary insight into Australian cities and/or Sydney was not available. It is surprising that the event failed to call upon urban sociologists, economists, and thinkers who are able to reveal incisive thinking about Sydney and emerging Australian cities. Also, Glaeser's raison d'etre of the city is almost too narrowly focused on economy (and not culture, history, or tradition), which is apparent from the sub-title of his book, *How Our Greatest Invention Makes Us Richer, Smarter, Healthier, and Happier*. It privileges a narrow, materialist point of view. Nevertheless, 'Urban Conversations' was a valuable and a well-attended event, and hopefully not just a one off.

2.7 Spatial Intelligence and New Domesticities: TEDxSydney 2012

TedXSydney commenced in 2010. It is described as a 'flagship TEDx event (one of a handful throughout the world that qualify as top tier for TED) that has already established itself as a platform and an ongoing pipeline for the propagation of Australian ideas, innovation and creativity to the widest possible global audience (TedxSydney, 2012)'. The event was held on the Saturday 26th May 2012 at the Carriage works in Redfern, and it featured three speakers from the University of Technology Sydney, who delivered two separate talks exploring the connection between design and urbanism— Anthony Burke (Associate Professor and Head of the School of Architecture, UTS); Gerard Reinmuth (Director of Architectural Practice TERROIR and Professor School of Architecture, UTS); and Tarsha Finney (Senior Lecturer, School of Architecture, UTS).

Burke and Reinmuth deliver the talk jointly and the topic is the profession and its practice. Burke commences by challenging the ideal and the unreal image of the architect, positioning her/him well within the links inside the network theory rather than above it, asking the audience to embrace disorder and dynamism in creative practice as the reality and the necessity. Burke goes onto argue that the architecture is 'mongrel not a thoroughbred,' suggesting the inevitability of complexity, diversity, and messiness (Burke and Reinmuth, 2012). This goes against the perceived image of the architect (Howard Roark in Fountainhead, the movie, 1949) and architecture (image of Villa Savoye, 1928–31, by Le Corbusier as the perfect example of a building standing pristine in its environment). Reinmuth emphasizes spatial thinking and intelligence, and he quotes Howard Gardener's inclusion of spatial intelligence as in his list of seven types of intelligence. Burke and Reinmuth maintain that every human being in equipped with this faculty, somehow diminished in capacity in adulthood but incredibly important to reawaken and foster if the design of the built environment were to be removed from the hands of the architects and placed in the custody and care of the people. Yet, Reinmuth notes, the planning of cities is located in the planning laws and documents, and silos of thought, without sophisticated spatial thinking tying it all together (Burke and Reinmuth, 2012).

Finney's talk on multi-residential housing highlights the discussion on the spatial knowledge of the city. Finney suggests that cities are fundamentally informed by cellular thinking. They are underpinned by the delineation of separate private and public spaces and a vast amount of resources are required to keep them separate. This is achieved by thinking of the city as a vast net that is radically held apart, keeping the fabric sparse, flat, and separate (Finney, 2012). Finney suggests that to be sustainable, we need to undermine separateness and consider density. Whilst she acknowledges the current trends in multi-residential housing, she suggests radically new ways of conceiving and inhabiting the domestic space, thereby expecting a level of agility in contemporary society. Finney (2012) cites examples of apartments that have not only shared laundries and pools, but also libraries that can be booked out by occupants who work from home. She suggests that another way of rethinking the domestic space might be to think of a shared commercial kitchen attached to one's dining room, to experiment and entertain—a virtual impossibility in a six-seater dining space setting. Finney (2012) closes by citing Kings Road House (1921) by Rudolph Schindler—a pinwheel organization shared by two young families that pivots around a central kitchen and a shared guest room. This is a prompt that suggests that rethinking domesticity is crucial to designing sustainable cities, which will not become possible through the consideration of density alone (Finney, 2012).

2.8 Building Sites: Weiss/Manfredi's Utzon Lecture at UNSW

Weiss/Manfredi (led by Marion Weiss and Michael Manfredi)—a New York City based multidisciplinary design practice known for their integration of architecture, art, infrastructure, and landscape design—delivered the Utzon Lecture Series Talk, *Inhabiting Topography*. Weiss/Manfredi has been awarded North America's Emerging Voices by the Architectural League of New York and the New York City American Institute of Architects Gold Medal of Honor. Opening the talk by acknowledging the debt to Romaldo Giurgola's scheme for Canberra (gained through Manfredi's experience at Mitchell/ Girugola in New York), they introduced the key idea underpinning their work: 'Sites are not given but made,' topographies are invented to foster public life; and that there is no such thing as the ideal site. The creation of the public realm then goes hand in hand with thinking of systems of drainage and flood patterns or highways and railways, thus giving rise to their approach—infrastructural topography.

Through the presentation of ten projects—Women's Memorial and Education Centre; Museum of the Earth; Smith College Campus Center; International Retreat; Barnard College Diana Center; Hunters Point South Waterfront Park; Taekwondo Park; Brooklyn Botanic Garden Visitor Center, Sylvan Grove; Seattle Art Museum; Olympic Sculpture Park—Weiss and Manfredi explained their approaches to the crafting of the public realm: Building as landscape and hence consisting of floor plates that slip in and out, over and under, to engage the peripheral vision of occupants; Juxtaposition of interior, exterior spaces, and in between spaces; Façade design that registers on the exterior surface; The changing quality of light during the day as well as deflects, transforms, and draws into the interior the light through glass walls, vertical mullions, shaded walkways and skylights; Introduction of a theatrical quality of seeing and being seen as the essence of occupying the landscape of urban life; and Sustainable strategies for combining aesthetic form of the ground and roof cover with its ethical performance by introducing water harvesting and solar panels.

Weiss and Manfredi close the talk by discussing the Seattle Art Museum, which was a complex and dynamic re-crafting of three disconnected sites (industrial site at the water's edge) through a process of folding back and forth down to the waterfront. The journey through the landscape stitches the fragmented sites together to provide the experience of sculptural art. What comes through very clearly in the presentation of their body of work is the blurring of disciplinary boundaries. Their work is committed to simultaneous agendas of ecology, infrastructure planning, urban design, landscape, architecture, and interior. It is not a box-ticking exercise, as all these commitments are filtered through community, identity, and local history, which gives the projects their civic orientation. The experiential dimension of their projects, notes Manfredi, is underpinned by a cinematic quality. This highlights not only the element of surprise and discovery, but also the dynamic, layered, and grafted quality of urban experience. Composed entirely a monochrome palette and forms that hark back to High Modernism, Weiss/Manfredi's projects are perhaps deliberately low on visual delight, as they provide the backdrop as well as the terrain for the performance of civic life, which is what animates their architecture.

Weiss and Manfredi's brief but meaningful contribution in Sydney and UNSW is well timed because Sydney (as well as design studios in the city's various Universities) is engaged with challenges and approaches pertaining to the crafting of public realms, the urgency of which is observable in the development of Central Park, now under construction and partially completed; launch of the Green Square Library & Plaza Design Competition; Design Parramatta, a collaborative project between Parramatta City Council and the NSW Government Architects Office; and more recently, Super Sydney that taps into people's vision of Sydney from the city's forty one council areas. Weiss/Manfredi's works are published in Marion Weiss and Michael Manfredi, Weiss/Manfredi: Surface/subsurface (New York: Princeton Architectural Press, 2008); Marion Weiss and Michael Manfredi, Site specific: The work of Weiss/Manfredi Architects (New York: Princeton Architectural Press, 2000).

References

Aston H (2012). MCA's Chequered Reception. *Sydney Morning Herald,* March 4. Available from: http://www.smh.com.au/nsw/mcas-chequered-reception-20120303-1u9n5.html [Accessed 29 April 2014].

Burke A and Reinmuth G (2012). Architecture, Gerard Reinmuth and Anthony Burke: TEDxSydney. Available from: http://www.youtube.com/watch?feature=player_embedded&v=TAkWq63zmR8 [Accessed 29 April 2014].

City of Sydney (2012a). *Architecture on Show: Small Spaces/Big Ideas*. Available from: http://whatson.cityofsydney.nsw.gov.au/events/13433-architecture-on-show-small-spaces-big-ideas [Accessed 29 April 2014].

Crawford B (2012). Planning Minister Wants Terraces, Not Big Blocks of Land. *The Sunday Telegraph* June 03. Available from: http://www.dailytelegraph.com.au/planning- minister-wants-terraces-not-big-blocks-of-land/story-e6freuy 9-1226381365956 [Accessed 29 April 2014].

Hazzard B (2013a). Press Release: More Housing Choices for Growth Centres August 28, 2013. Available from: www.planning.nsw.gov.au [Accessed 29 April 2014].

Farrelly E (2012a). Spatial Delight Gets Lost at MCA. *Sydney Morning Herald,* March 27. Available from: http://www.smh.com.au/federal-politics/society-and-culture/spatial-delight-gets-lost-at-mca-20120326-1vup9.html [Accessed 29 April 2014].

Farrelly E (2012b). Bold, Frank Criticism can only Nourish Architecture. *Sydney Morning Herald,* May 10. Available from: http://www.smh.com.au/federal-politics/political-opinion/bold-frank-criticism-can-only-nourish-architecture-20120509-1ycxm.html [Accessed 29 April 2014].

Finney T (2012). Share More Space: Tarsha Finney at TEDxSydney. Available from: http://www.youtube.com/watch?feature=player_embedded&v=Abm6dMtcQeA [Accessed 29 April 2014].

Historic Houses Trust (2012a). Sydney Open Talks: House. Previously available from: http://www.hht.net.au/whats_on/event/architecture/sydney_open_lecture_series; [Accessed 19 May 2012].

Historic Houses Trust (2012b). Sydney Open Talks: House. Previously available from: http://www.hht.net.au/discover/highlights/articles/sydney_open_talks_house_bios#terrace [Accessed 19 May 2012].

Johanson S (2011). Australian Homes Still the World's Biggest. Sydney Morning Herald, August 22. Available from: http://www.smh.com.au/business/property/australian-homes-still-the-worlds-biggest-20110822-1j5ev.html [Accessed 29 April 2014].

Make Space for Architecture (2014). About. Available from: http://www.ms4a.org/about-2/. [Accessed 29 April 2014].

Neuman M (2012a). *Sticks and Stones will make my Bones: Utzon Lecture.* Available from: http://www.be.unsw.edu.au/content/2012-utzon-lecture-series-fifth-annual-paul-reid-lecture-urban-design [Accessed 29 April 2014].

Neuman M (2012b). *Sticks and Stones will make my Bones,* Video. Available from: http://www.youtube.com/watch?v=plwOGXaJB14&feature=player_embedded#! [Accessed 29 April 2014].

Neustein D (2012). MCA: Open Conversation or Guarded Debate? *Australian Design Review,* 04 May. Available from: http://www.australiandesignreview.com/opinion/19562-mca-open-conversation-or-guarded-debate [Accessed 29 April 2014].

Ooi T (2011). NSW Planning and Infrastructure Minister Brad Hazzard Vows to Cut Red Tape for Housing Builders. *TheAustralian,* October 06. Available from: http://www.theaustralian.com.au/business/property/minister-vows-to-cut-red-tape-for-housing-builders/story-fn9656lz-1226159544370 [Accessed 29 April 2014].

Reinmuth G (2012). Critical Thinking *Australian Design Review,* 07 May. Available from: http://www.australiandesignreview.com/opinion/19584-critical-thinking [Accessed 29 April 2014].

Serisier G (2012). Lines of Division: The New MCA in Sydney. *Australian Design Review,* 09 May. Available from: http://www.australiandesignreview.com/opinion/19607-lines-of-division-the-new-mca-in-sydney [Accessed 29 April 2014].

Tedx Sydney, http://www.tedxsydney.com/assets/documents/tedxsydney2012.pdf

Chapter 03
New Public Domains

Abstract: New Public Domains presents a look at the ongoing development of the civic spaces and institutions in Sydney. The term 'public domain' is used instead of public space or civic buildings, to discuss libraries, cafes, museums, parks, and infrastructure projects within the ambit of this chapter. At the level of the city, it seems that the formation and re-formation of Sydney is continuous, and the projects that stand out are the ones that negotiate public good with private profit and ownership.

Key words: Landscape urbanism, urban design, sustainable transport, liveability

3.1 Introduction

New Public Domains presents a look at the ongoing development of the civic spaces and institutions in Sydney. The term 'public domain' is used instead of public space or civic buildings, to discuss libraries, cafes, museums, parks, and infrastructure projects within the ambit of this chapter. At the level of the city, it seems that the formation and re-formation of Sydney is continuous, and the projects that stand out are the ones that negotiate public good with private profit and ownership. In addition to the ones presented in this chapter, the other ones not discussed here are the East Darling Harbour, Darling Quarter (ASPECT Studios with FJMT Architects) Destination Sydney led by Lend Lease with HASSELL, OMA and Populous) which is a 'redevelopment of the Sydney Entertainment Centre, Convention Centre and Exhibition Centre at Darling Harbour,' or the more recently commissioned Goods Line which is being designed and led by ASPECT Studios with CHROFI for the Sydney Harbour Foreshore Authority (Australian Design Review, 2012; ASPECT Studios, 2014a).

Sydney's New Downtown, known as the Central Park, is the newest most prominent urban renewal development in inner city. It can be argued though that despite featuring leading architects from Sydney and overseas and aggressive and effective marketing, Central Park inescapably captures the phenomenon of 'brandscapes,' providing a mixture of desirable and recognizable elements without a unifying logic authentic to the place. A *'Field Approach'* uncovers a perceptive take on public space informing the winning competition entry for the Green Square Library and Plaza. The originality of the scheme is that it moves away from formal integrity of public buildings and their separateness from the life outside the building, integrating study with play, open with closed, architecture with landscape.

Urban Protocols will outline the detailed and complex set of guidelines and approaches for excellence in urban design advocated by the Department of Infrastructure and Regional Development. Far from being a didactic set of rules, the protocols are a synthesis of policies at state and national levels, exemplified by case studies of recent award winning projects. *Light Rail* and *Bike Hub* also address Sydney's interest in integrating the fragmented public realm. The projects not only fulfil the infrastructural demands of the city, but also mount a challenge to the colonisation and fracturing of the public space by the car, and the increasing volume of traffic in an urbanizing city.

3.2 A 'Field Approach': Winning Scheme for Green Square Library and Plaza Design Competition

The competition for one of the most coveted projects by City of Sydney—the Green Square Library and Plaza—received the submission of 167 entries from local as well as international practices. The Library and the Plaza are set within the Green Square project redevelopment area of '278 hectares [which]...includes the suburbs of Beaconsfield and Zetland, and parts of Rosebery, Alexandria, and Waterloo.' Located 'just 3.5 km from the city centre and 4 km from the airport,' Green Square is thus an ideal location to create new areas of work, living, and leisure as well as densify inner city. The City of Sydney notes: 'By 2030, Green Square is expected to attract 40,000 new residents and 22,000 new workers (City of Sydney, 2014a).' It is within this context that the Library and Plaza becomes an anchor project.

Figure 18 Green Square Library and Plaza, view from Botany Road looking east to the Entry Triangle and Library Tower, Project: Stewart Hollenstein with Colin Stewart Architects [Image: Luxigon]

One needs to only look at the website http://sydneyyoursay.com.au/greensquare to see the range of proposals that explore the idea of the library as an urban living room in contemporary society. This is indebted to the notion of the third space (introduced first in 1989 by American urban sociologist, Ray Oldenburg) becomes increasingly significant as the humane places of belonging, identity, socialization and networking, outside of home and away from work. Libraries as urban living rooms is given more currency due to the changes in the way information is stored, disseminated and shared, thereby acknowledging electronic media and content as drivers of change. This is recognized in the Jury's report, which reiterates this as part of the Green Square Competition brief:

> An exploration of the importance and meaning of 'the library' is central to this project. The library, as a building type, has been evolving throughout time. Initially a repository of books and documents, and a place to access the information and knowledge contained within, libraries also became community hubs, and places to engage with others. With the recent rapid changes in technology, people's ability to access information has changed but the library still exists as a physical place to have access to knowledge and to engage with other people (City of Sydney, 2014b, p4).

The idea of the living room is recognized here, as the brief also indicates the need for an appropriately programmed outdoor public space. The report states that the plaza will be a place for the community—a place to gather, to linger, to dine and shop. It will be capable of accommodating public events and markets, as well as day-to-day practicalities such as shade and shelter and conversely, places to enjoy sunshine. The plaza design will respond to the site's complex geometry, as well as resolve the competing demands of outdoor dining, pedestrian and vehicular movement, and service easements (City of Sydney, 2014b, p4).

Figure 19 Green Square Library and Plaza, View from an adjacent apartment looking down over the plaza, Project: Stewart Hollenstein with Colin Stewart Architects [Image: Luxigon]

The brief is positioned within the context of a high demand for designed public domains in Sydney—an imperative that informs almost all completed as well as upcoming projects like Central Park; redesign of George Street; and re-structuring of Central Station Precinct.

The accomplished jury of Glenn Murcutt (Multiple award-winning Australian architect and 2002 Pritzker Prize winner), George Hargreaves (International Urban Designer and Landscape Architect from USA), Rachel Neeson (award winning Architect and Adjunct Professor, University of Sydney), Sharan Harvey (Manager of Brisbane City Council Library Services) and Stuart McCreery (Structural Engineer with Evans & Peck) and chaired by John Denton selected Stewart Hollenstein with Colin Stewart Architects, Sydney, JPE Design, Adelaide; John Wardle Architects, Melbourne; Flannery de la Pole, UK; and Felix Laboratories, Fremantle to proceed to Stage 2 of the competition. This is a commissioned invited design competition, distinct from Stage 1, which is open anonymous design competition. The Stage 2 scheme by Stewart Hollenstein with Colin Stewart Architects was judged as the winning design (City of Sydney, 2014b, p9, 14). The Jury notes:

> It was the only scheme to challenge the notion of placing a building in the Plaza, managing to put forward a strong argument for placing the Plaza over the Library, thereby providing both a building and a suitably scaled urban plaza for the future developments around the site, becoming a beacon and an oasis for the whole Green Square community. The Jury responded positively to how this scheme would maximise the opportunity for sunlight into the entire Plaza area.

> The single-level library creates an efficiency of planning, punctuated by 'pop-up' and 'cut-out' elements that express themselves at Plaza level. The single level, generally open-plan library and the 'field approach' for the Plaza with scattered elements across the site was found to be a robust strategy that would be able to accommodate rigorous design development without significant change to the substance of the idea (City of Sydney, 2014b, p20).

City of Sydney notes that while some of the 'buildings are below ground while bookshelves sit outdoors in the plaza. The design includes an amphitheatre, a storytelling garden, water play zone and wide open spaces for festivals.' Undoubtedly, the 'design redefines the traditional idea of a library, fusing a range of innovative buildings with the outdoor plaza to create multiple sites for play, work, and rest (City of Sydney, 2014c).'

Whilst the scheme rethinks the typology of the library, the key winning point is really that it engages the new approach to landscape urbanism. Ian Hamilton Thompson's 'Ten Tenets and Six Questions for Landscape Urbanism (2012)' is a useful starting point. The winning scheme by Stewart Hollenstein with Colin Stewart Architects begins to attend to some of these tenets, by challenging the enduring classical typology of the building in a square. The scheme attends to the tenets 1 ('Landscape Urbanism Rejects the Binary Opposition Between City and Landscape') and 9 ('Landscape Urbanism Encourages Hybridity between Natural and Engineered Systems') by undermining the distinction between figure and ground, mass and surface, building and landscape, and by using pop ups and cuts outs and figuring the library partially below ground. The scheme attends to tenet 2 ('Landscape Replaces Architecture as the Basic Building Block of Cities') and 4 ('Landscape Urbanism Prepares Fields for Action and Stages for Performances') by allowing the landscape elements such as the play zone, spaces for festivals and storytelling garden to guide the scheme. The scheme is a timely response to the shift in emphasis from architecture to urbanism or architecture + urbanism, which informs the Jury's qualification of the scheme as 'a great library for the future (City of Sydney, 2014b, p21).'

3.3 Urban Protocols

One of the recent initiatives of the Australian Government is the *Creating Places for People: Urban Design Protocol for Australian Cities* forum, which seeks to delineate and promote quality of planning and design measures across multiples scales of the built environment as well as regions. The key agenda is stated as follows:

> *Creating Places* for People—an urban design protocol for Australian cities (the Protocol) establishes twelve broadly agreed principles for quality urban places in the Australian context. These principles can be applied to any project or location—whether it is in a large capital city, regional centre or rural town (Department of Infrastructure and Regional Development, Australia, 2014a).

The protocol has relationships to national- and state-level policies and guidelines for urban design and is supported by several governmental and non-governmental. The twelve principles are spread across three distinctive bands of relevance: 'Design Principles about Place: Productivity + Sustainability,' 'Design Principles about People: Liveability,' and 'Principles about Leadership and Governance (Department of Infrastructure and Regional Development, Australia, 2014b).'

'Design Principles about Place' includes the principles of enhancing the local community, economy, and environment, focussing on strengthening the aspects of the built environment that are already working. 'Connected' addresses the issue of link and continuity between past and present, between places of work and play, between built and natural environment, and between various modes of transport. 'Diverse' addresses the range of experiences and options for housing, shopping, and leisure that people can access depending on their interest, budget, and capacity (Department of Infrastructure and Regional Development, Australia, 2014b). 'Enduring' is to do with the building of resilient places and structures that optimize on energy and materials that can be easily maintained or cared for. 'Design Principles about People' addresses the issue of creating comfortable spaces that can be accessed and enjoyed equally by people from different ages and capacities, without necessarily having to pay to use it. It also seeks to create spaces that are vibrant and safe, above all walkable and not governed by the use of car, promoting a healthier lifestyle (Department of Infrastructure and Regional Development, Australia, 2014b). 'Principles about Leadership and Governance' emphasize the importance of working within the context of place, planning frameworks, history and heritage. These also highlight the importance of engagement with important stakeholders in creating places that are employing best practice standards and universal design as well as maintenance and custodianship over time (Department of Infrastructure and Regional Development, Australia, 2014b). The protocol document also clarifies the meanings of key terms: 'Urban structure,' 'Urban grain,' 'Density + mix,' 'Height + massing,' 'Streetscape + landscape,' 'Facade + interface,' 'Details + materials,' 'Public Realm,' 'Topography, landscape,' and 'Social + economic fabric.'

Creating Places for People suggests Darling Quarters (winner of 2012 Australia Award for Urban Design), Parramatta River Urban Design Strategy (winner of 2012 Australia Award for Urban Design), and Paddington Reservoir Gardens (winner of 2009 Australia Award for Urban Design) in Sydney. The collaboration of Lend Lease, FJMT, and ASPECT Studios creates a public place that far exceeds a mere satisfactory response to the 12 points of the protocol. The precinct features a range of retail spaces, with cafes and restaurants, a 300-seat children's theatre, an innovative playground as its centre piece, and 4,000 sq m illuminated playground, with two new six-star rated commercial buildings (Commonwealth Bank Place). It attends to some key issues: 'Re-vitalisation of the western edge of the Sydney CBD,' and integrating the 'new project into the existing precinct so it reads as an enlargement of the existing public domain (Department of Infrastructure and Regional Development, Australia, 2014c).' ASPECT Studios points out two new pedestrian connections. One is the 'civic connector' that 'connects Tumbalong Park to Bathurst street and Town Hall,' and the other is the 'pedestrian link—the Pedestrian Boulevard [that] reinforces the movement between the Entertainment Centre, Cockle Bay and beyond and prioritises the pedestrian connections through the site (ASPECT Studios, 2014b).'

Parramatta River Urban Design Strategy is a regeneration project across 31 hectares encompassing Parramatta CDB and waterfront. Led by McGregor Coxall (in collaboration with Equatica) for the Parramatta City Council, the project most importantly 'reorientates the Parramatta's CBD towards the river and positions Parramatta Quay as a new water-arrival point in the heart of Parramatta, connecting Parramatta's CBD to Circular Quay by ferry (Department of Infrastructure and Regional Development, Australia, 2014d).' The principles of vibrancy and connectedness of the protocol are addressed, with some key moves including the relocation of Charles Street Weir and Parramatta Quay, suggesting a new centre and a new orientation towards the river; creation of connections like 'Civic Place' that connect the CBD to the river; design of promenades and square for an active enjoyment of the riverfront, or 'waterside terraces' for a more passive absorption of the river and a view of the ferries. Nevertheless, what is also striking is that the commitment to the principle of creating enduring and resilient places, especially here where is a strong focus on the restoration and maintenance of river ecology through the 'water cycle management (Department of Infrastructure and Regional Development, Australia, 2014d).'

3.4 Sydney's New Downtown Central Park

Central Park, a 2 billion dollars urban village developed by Frasers Property and Sekisui House, aims to deliver 'Sydney's new Downtown' that will provide Sydneysiders with opportunities to live, work and shop (Central Park, 2013a). The master plan is developed by Jean Nouvel, Johnson Pilton Walker (JPW), and Fosters and Partners, with Tzannes Associates. With '11 buildings, around 2,000 apartments and a lively collection of shops, cafes, restaurants, laneways, terraces and offices,' specifically 2500 residential occupants and 5400 working population in the commercial and retail spaces, Central Park addresses Sydney's push for high density environments (Central Park, 2013b). The emphasis on density is recent, emerging out of the recognition of the impacts of urban sprawl, and the knowledge that density underpins urbanism that is sustainable, vital, and engaged. Central Park also responds to the need for successful public domains, which according to many leading urban designers are far and few in Sydney for the lack of clear vision in the history of its planning. The precinct, therefore, consists of residential, retail, and commercial space planned around a spacious urban park of 6,400 square meters, complemented by a network of roads and pathways generating a new urban fabric at the heart of inner city.

Central Park is an outcome of rational master planning and the collaboration of accomplished local and international practices. It consists of three high-rise developments. *One Central Park* by Jean Nouvel with

PTW Architects consists of two 'residential towers rising above a retail centre, connected by terraced gardens to the main park beyond (Central Park, 2013c).' *Park Lane* by JPW highlights the typical urban experience of overlooking the expansive space of a leafy green park, as an 'intimate paved laneway' separates the two buildings, one which is a 'low-rise building directly facing the park' and the other is a 'lofty tower with views to park and city (Central Park, 2013d).' Mark by JPW, a residential building, is a 'soaring glass tower of great presence' consisting of two apartment groups separated vertically (Mark 1 from levels 1–19, and Mark 2 from levels 20–27). With the 'exterior that could move and change and excite' and its resolved proportion and vertical ascent, Mark is important as an urban icon (Central Park, 2013e). At the base of One Central Park is a 'naturally lit six floor retail mall—*Central*—that brings superior youth shopping and services to this urban village (think Tokyo with its layers of micro boutiques and quirky fashion outlets) serving locals and students alike with a creative hum that continues well into the evening (Central Park, 2013f).' The Old Brewery building (retained and adapted by Tzannes Associates to new uses such as retail, micro-brewery and cafes and restaurants) and the Chippendale Green form the heart of the precinct. The eastern boundary of Central Park is Kensington Street (Tonkin Zulaikha Greer for master planning and adaptive reuse of the heritage buildings), and the Abercrombie Street development by Foster and Partners provides student housing alongside what is termed as the 'commercial campus (Central Park, 2013g).'

Lisa McCutchion, the group marketing manager, provides an insight into the development of this precinct. She notes that the site was an island in the middle of Chippendale and the purpose of the master plan was to integrate this to the existing fabric with major pedestrian and cycle ways through the site and moving parking underground with no parking at the heart of the site. The master plan is also informed by the attention to the street edge on Broadway so the mass of the built fabric is moved from the centre to the edge with the Art deco heritage hotels marking the edges of the precinct. McCutchion notes how the master plan is structured to protect the development from Broadway, as it were, and reveal it from the side of Chippendale. The master planning is done to respond to the varying social, physical, and cultural aspects of its different edges.

Alec Tzannes, director of Tzannes Associates who played a key role in shaping the master plan, notes that the 'master plan is the unifying element that dictates the overall design, resulting in buildings that are memorable and distinctive, and enjoys a more special relationship with the people who inhabit them (Central Park, 2013f).' This principle can be evidenced in the fact that each project has a distinctive identity in the overall scheme. One Central Park has the vertical gardens designed by Patrick Blanc, and the Heliostat composed of stainless steel panels attached to the underside of the cantilevered Sky Garden that intend to reflect light through to the retail atrium below. At night, the heliostat 'transforms into a monumental piece of public art, with almost 3000 coloured LED lights creating a dazzling light display designed by French lighting artist, YannKersale (Central Park, 2013g).' Park Lane emphasizes the domestic character of view of an immediate landscape, laneways, and fine grain texture of apartment emphasizing encounter, intimacy, and neighbourliness. Mark works mostly as an urban icon.

Peeling back the layers of positivist descriptions of the project reveals that the master plan is interesting because it utilizes a range of functional and formal typologies—the green building and the vertical garden; the terrace in the park; the tower as an urban beacon, and the urban park. In other words, Central Park presents a microcosm of the city, like a city within the city, strongly reminiscent of Leon Krier's 1977 essay of the same name:

> A city can only be reconstructed in the form of urban quarters. A large or a small city can only be reorganized as a large or a small number of urban quarters; as a federation of autonomous quarters. Each quarter must have its own center, periphery, and limit. Each quarter must be A CITY WITHIN A CITY. The quarter must integrate all daily functions of urban life (dwelling, working, leisure) within a territory dimensioned on the basis of the comfort of a walking person; not exceeding 35 hectares (80 acres) in surface and 15,000 inhabitants….(Krier, 1977, p.69).

Krier's theory was rejected for being 'reductive and ultimately meaningless' by Manuel Castells, and for being a form of environmental determinism, and Central Park suffers from a similar artifice complex. In this new downtown, it is now possible to experience the city in an edited form without really traversing the city, with its wastelands and sprawl. In bearing resemblance to Weissenhofsiedlung housing estate built in Stuttgart in 1927, Central Park evokes the air of optimism, an open air laboratory or gallery of twenty-first century Australian dreams of high rise, sustainability, and the citification of Sydney.

3.5 Light Rail: Adaptive Reuse of Transport Infrastructure

In December 2012 the New South Wales (NSW) Government announced the construction of the light rail from Sydney CBD to Randwick and Kingsford. The much-awaited transport link will run from Circular Quay down George Street to Central, and then on to the Sydney Cricket Ground and Allianz Stadium, Randwick Racecourse, the University of NSW (UNSW) and the Prince of Wales Hospital at Randwick. Estimated to cost $1.6 billion, the light rail venture is part of the *NSW Long Term Transport Master Plan*—an overall plan which seeks to guide the development of an integrated, modern transport system that will support the State's economic and social growth over a period 20 years (Transport for NSW, 2012a; Transport for NSW, 2012b). Included within the Transport Master Plan is a long-term action plan—*Sydney's Light Rail Future*—a plan that seeks to extend the existing light rail network within the Sydney CBD to the inner Sydney areas (Transport for NSW, 2012b).

It forms the basis for the proposed 12 kilometre light rail project to the south eastern suburbs, and the 5.6 kilometre Inner West Light Rail Extension that is currently under construction and will extend the light rail services from Lilyfield to the inner western suburbs of Dulwich Hill, Leichhardt and Haberfield (Transport for NSW, 2012a). The light rail is considered to be a solution that will help greatly reduce traffic congestion within the CBD while catering to the growing need for public transport in a sustainable and effective manner. As compared to buses which carry a maximum of 100 people, each light rail will be able to move across 300 people, thereby reducing buses in the CDB and lowering congestion. Furthermore, it is believed that as in the case of cities like Barcelona, Dublin, Zurich, Melbourne, Istanbul, San Francisco, Nottingham, Strasbourg and Manchester, the extension of the light rail system in Sydney will aid in the urban renewal of the city as it will support higher density living and will encourage the creation of public spaces, shops, cafes and restaurants, thereby revitalizing parts of the urban and suburban fabric (Transport for NSW, 2012a).

The Randwick and Kingsford light rail is being viewed as a 'catalyst for urban renewal' in the Randwick Urban Activation Precinct which includes the local centres of the suburbs of Kingsford, Kensington and Randwick (NSW Planning & Infrastructure, 2012). Following deliberations and community and stakeholders consultations held through early and mid-2013, the NSW Government has identified the areas of Randwick and Anzac Parade South as two precincts in the area which are considered as having the potential for urban renewal. The precincts are perceived as presenting a 'unique opportunity to carry out integrated planning for additional homes and employment in the area to be serviced by the future light rail,' and are part of a larger housing supply program initiated by the NSW Government of providing up to 172,000 new homes to be delivered across the greater Sydney area (Hazzard, 2013b).

While the more obvious advantages of the light rail system are quite well established, perhaps it's most viable, yet under-explored aspects are that it represents a unique opportunity for the adaptive reuse of abandoned transport infrastructure. This includes rail and tram corridors that were once active in the inner west and in the eastern suburbs. The existing light rail service between Wentworth Park and Lilyfield which was constructed in 1996 uses the former Darling Harbour goods line, and the inner west extension currently under construction employs the former Rozelle freight corridor that was established in 1916 (Transport for NSW, 2012 b). The light rail to the south-east will run along the tramways along Anzac Parade which was once an active transport corridor for trams from the city all the way to La Perouse. These former transport networks greatly supported the expansion of Sydney and the growth of industry in the inner city areas during the nineteenth and the early twentieth centuries. At its peak during the 1930s Sydney's trams network was the largest in Australia covering a distance a total route distance of 368 km with up to 1570 cars, handling 429 million passengers per year (Improve Sydney Public Transport). While the closure of the freight lines was understandably brought about by the decentralization of industry away from inner city areas, the highly effective tramways were also affected, and more so as the city continued to expand out west—a move that was fuelled by the increasing use and dependence on the private car, as public transport to the newer suburbs failed to meet growing needs. The last tram in Sydney operated in 1961, and buses which were seen as the more cost effective and flexible alternative to the fixed track system of the trams, soon replaced all the trams often running along the established tram routes (Wotherspoon, 2008).

While the former tram systems were plagued by issues of economy, safety and efficiency, the light rail system, which has been operational and in use in Europe and the United States since the early 1970s, is a system that is intended for light loads, faster movement and lesser investment in infrastructure than a traditional train or tram system. Furthermore it has also been demonstrated through the cases of a number of European cities such as the German city of Karlsruhe and the Flemish city of Hasselt that the introduction of the light rail helps create more liveable, accessible and interactive urban spaces as it forms part of the public realm of streets and squares, and is seen as a way of reclaiming back space in city from the car (Houthaeve, 2009). It is hoped that with the introduction of the light rail, Sydney will be able to develop a more integrated transport system in which the light rail will act as a link between bus and train networks, and by doing so it will not only enable the revitalization of the fabric of the city but will also aid in the reinstalment of its former vast tram network.

3.6 Taylor Square: Sydney's First Bicycle Hub

At the intersection of Flinders Street and Oxford Street, Surry Hills is Taylor Square—one of Sydney's most well-known landmark locations. This is the site for the first proposed bicycle hub in Sydney—a recognition of the growing numbers of cyclists in the city. Part of the City of Sydney Council's 'vision to restore Taylor Square to a people-friendly precinct…to activate the area to make it more lively, attractive, and safe,' the cycle hub will be situated within and around the heritage listed former Commonwealth Bank building which occupies this intersection (Clover Moore cited in Bibby, 2010). In fact the reactivation of Taylor Square has recently involved the City of Sydney's City Art Program which included two works of public art installed on either sides of the Square. The work of Aboriginal Australian artist Reko Rennie titled *Always Was Always Will Be* currently occupies the façade of the former bank building, whereas the WindGrid—the work of British artist Tim Knowles had occupied the opposite, northern side of the Square.

Since its formation in the early 1900s, Taylor Square has been one of the busiest intersections in the city, and continues to be a widely used public meeting space for pedestrians and cyclist with three cycle routes and a separated cycleway congregating at the junction. Therefore it is fitting that the bicycle hub as a symbol of the increasing awareness of the need for alternative and sustainable means of transport, will occupy this historic site. The hub is one of the series of similar projects being promoted by the City of Sydney's Sustainable Sydney 2030 Plan which seeks to reduce the carbon footprint of the city (Hassell, 2012). Recognising that the number of bike trips has doubled in the last 3 years, and that an average 31,600 people living within its boundaries use a bike in a typical week, the City of Sydney hopes to create a 200 kilometre network of bicycle tracks integrated with roadways (City of Sydney). The aim is to encourage people to choose cycling as a safe, sustainable and healthier means of transport, thereby cutting down automobile dependency. Other initiatives that support bike riders include series of bike-riding and bike-maintenance courses organised and run by the City of Sydney, and its ongoing support for major cycling festivals and events every year.

In 2012 the City of Sydney invited tenders for the $3.8 million bicycle hub and after having received and reviewed 27 submissions the project was awarded to Hassell—an international design practice (Fedele, 2012). Hassell has prior experience in designing for cyclist venues, with its recent design for the vertical 'hanging tree' storage system for London. Drawing upon similar vertical stacking systems employed in Japan, Switzerland and Iran, Hassell has designed vertical storage towers which will allow cyclists to securely store their bikes on city streets (Hassell, 2013). The Taylor Square bike hub project when compared to the 'tighter' constraints of the London project, offers Hassell a larger canvas to work with. Their proposed design has accordingly included master planning for the future upgrade of the public square, along with the proposed adaptive reuse of the former bank building (Hassell, 2012). The building which was built in the mid-1900s is a three-storeyed Federation period structure that has heritage significance as it represents a phase in the historic development of the city, and forms an important part of the existing streetscape. It will be refurbished internally and externally, so as to create community and social spaces which will be part of the surrounding square. The bike hub will provide a community venue for cyclists and pedestrians, and will include retail, information and service facilities (Hassell, 2012).

Once completed the bike hub will reactivate Taylor Square and its surrounds including the environs of Oxford Street. However more importantly through the proposed reuse of the heritage listed building and the emphasis on encouraging and supporting more people to cycle, the bike hub project will demonstrates a deliberate and conscious move towards sustainability and a more environmentally sensitive use of built environment resources.

References

Aspect Studios (2014a).Goods Line. Available from: http://aspect.net.au/?cat=9 [Accessed 29 April 2014].

Australian Design Review (2012). HASSELL, OMA, Populous to Redevelop Syd Entertainment Precinct, Australian Design Review, 11 December. Available from: http://www.australiandesignreview.com/news/26824-hassell-oma-to-redevelop-sydney-entertainment-precinct [Accessed 29 April 2014].

City of Sydney (2014a). Green Square. Available from: http://www.cityofsydney.nsw.gov.au/vision/major-developments/green-square [Accessed 29 April 2014].

City of Sydney (2014b). Green Square Library & Plaza Design Competition Jury Report. Available from: http://www.cityofsydney.nsw.gov.au/__data/assets/pdf_file/0006/194712/GreenSqLibraryDesignComp_JuryReport_WEB.pdf [Accessed 29 April 2014].

City of Sydney (2014c). Green Square: The Winner is. Available from: http://www.cityofsydney.nsw.gov.au/vision/major-developments/green-square/the-winner-is [Accessed 29 April 2014].

Thompson IH (2012). 'Ten Tenets and Six Questions for Landscape Urbanism,' Landscape Research, 37:1, 7-26

Department of Infrastructure and Regional Development, Australia (2014a). *Creating Places for People: Urban Design Protocol for Australian Cities*. Available from: http://www.urbandesign.gov.au/introduction/index.aspx [Accessed 29 April 2014].

Department of Infrastructure and Regional Development, Australia (2014b). *Creating Places for People: Urban Design Protocol for Australian Cities*. Available from: http://www.urbandesign.gov.au/downloads/files/INFRA1219_MCU_R_SQUARE_URBAN_PROTOCOLS_1111_WEB_FA2.pdf [Accessed 29 April 2014].

Department of Infrastructure and Regional Development, Australia (2014c). *Creating Places for People: Urban Design Protocol for Australian Cities*. Available from: http://www.urbandesign.gov.au/casestudies/darling.aspx

Aspect Studios (2014b). Darling Quarter. Available from: http://aspect.net.au/?p=361 [Accessed 29 April 2014].

Department of Infrastructure and Regional Development, Australia (2014d). Available from: http://www.urbandesign.gov.au/casestudies/parramatta.aspx. [Accessed 29 April 2014].

Central Park (2013a). Sydney's New Downtown. Available from: http://www.centralparksydney.com [Accessed 15 July 2013].

Central Park (2013b). Available from: http://www.central parksydney.com/about-the-project/ [Accessed 15 July 2013].

Central Park (2013c). One Central Park Available from: http://www.centralparksydney.com [Accessed 15 July 2013].

Central Park (2013d). Park Lane. Available from: http://www.centralparksydney.com/park-lane/ [Accessed 15 July 2013].

Central Park (2013e). Available from: http://www.central parksydney.com/architecture-3/ [Accessed 15 July 2013].

Central Park (2013f). Available from: http://www.central parksydney.com/amenities-2/ [Accessed 15 July 2013].

Central Park (2013). Available from: http://www.centralparksy dney.com/abercrombie-street/ [Accessed 15 July 2013].

Central Park (2013f). Available from: http://www.central parksydne.com/masterplan/ [Accessed 15 July 2013].

Central Park (2013g). Available from: http://www.central parksydney.com/heliostat-floats-above-broadway/ [Accessed 15 July 2013].

Leon Krier, A+ U, Tokyo, Special Issue, November 1977, pages 69–152. Reprinted in: *Architectural Design*, volume 54 (1984), Jul/Aug pages 70–105.

Transport for NSW (2012a). NSW Long Term Transport Master Plan. Available from: http://www.transport.nsw.gov.au/sites/default/files/b2b/publications/nsw-transport-masterplan-final.pdf [Accessed 15 July 2013].

Transport for NSW (2012b). Sydney's Light Rail Future: Expanding Public Transport, Revitalising our City. Available from: http://www.transport.nsw.gov.au/sites/default/files/b2b/projects/Sydneys_Light_Rail_Future_December_2012.pdf [Accessed 15 July 2013].

NSW Planning & Infrastructure (2012), Randwick Urban Activation Precinct. Available from: http://www.planning.nsw.gov.au/en-us/deliveringhomes/urbanactivation/randwick.aspx [Accessed 15 July 2013].

Hazzard, B (2013b). Press Release: Urban Renewal Aligned to Light Rail, March 18, 2013, Available from: www.planning.nsw.gov.au [Accessed 29 April 2014].

Improve Sydney Public Transport, n.d. Tramway Statics. Available from: http://www.isput.com.au/wp-content/uploads/tramstats.pdf. [Accessed 09 May 2014].

Wotherspoon G. (2008). 'Trams,' Dictionary of Sydney. Available from: http://www.dictionaryofsydney.org/entry/trams [Accessed 09 May 2014].

Houthaeve R. (2009). 'Light Rail Provides a Design for a Healthy and Liveable Urban Public Space' presented at 45th ISOCARP Congress. Available from: http://www.isocarp.net/data/case_studies/1592.pdf [Accessed 09 May 2014].

Bibby P. (2010). 'Wheel Turns for Notorious Pub,' Sydney Morning Herald, January 26. Available from: http://www.smh.com.au/national/wheel-turns-for-notorious-pub-20100125-mukh.html [Accessed 09 May 2014].

Hassell (2012). 'HASSELL set to transform Taylor Square South into Sydney's First Bike Hub,' 13 December. Available from: http://www.hassellstudio.com/en/cms-news/hassell-set-to-transform-taylor-square-south-into-sydneys-first-bike-hub. [Accessed 09 May 2014].

Hassell (2013). 'HASSELL Designs London Cycle Superhub,' 28 March. Available from: http://www.hassellstudio.com/en/cms-news/hassell-designs-london-cycle-superhub> [Accessed 09 May 2014].

Fedele A. (2012). 'Iconic Taylor Square to Become Sydney's First Bike Hub,' *DesignBuild Source*, 19 December. Available from: http://cyclingresourcecentre.org.au/news/iconic_taylor_square_to_become_sydneys_first_bike_hub. [Accessed 09 May 2014].

City of Sydney (2013d). Cycling. Available from: www.cityofsydney.nsw.gov.au/explore/getting-around/cycling. [Accessed 09 May 2014].

Chapter 04

Immersive Installations and Public Art

Abstract: *Immersive Installations and Public Art* is a look at a very vast arts/architecture scene in Sydney. There are many architectural practitioners who lead a parallel professional life, experimenting with new technologies, materials, relational philosophies by designing/building temporary or permanent interiors, installations, and public art. Not only does this tell you something about the wider domain of design thinking which transcends typology, scale, and material but also that the professional practice has some inherent limitations and rigid boundaries.

Key words: Immersive, public art, interactive/responsive installation

4.1 Introduction

Immersive Installations and Public Art is a look at a very vast arts/architecture scene in Sydney. There are many architectural practitioners who lead a parallel professional life, experimenting with new technologies, materials, relational philosophies by designing/building temporary or permanent interiors, installations, and public art. Similarly, there are artists whose works are architectural in the sense that they address spatiality, place, enclosure, and the city. The opportunities for this are again provided by the various festivals (Vivid, Design Week, Sydney Architecture Festivals, Sydney Festival, Art and About Festival); university exhibitions; design associations and institutions (Powerhouse Museum, Object Gallery, Customs House, Australian Institute of Architects); public art opportunities in city councils like City of Sydney, City of Penrith; City of Parramatta; Architecture and Design Associations; or non-profit organizations or collectives like Expanded Architecture.

The parallel practice of art/architecture is a hybrid field of stage set design, installations, public art, lighting design, immersive interiors, and so on is very important. Notwithstanding the discipline or the typology of the project, these practitioners are concerned with two interrelated issues—first is the human figure, specifically the sensory faculties, and second is the designing or bringing forth of the immaterial (in the material). Whether it is memory, history, race, imagination, or nature (organic or inorganic), the immersive qualities of these constructions highlight the human through the immaterial. These projects almost always figure new collaborations, across practices and disciplines, keeping open the field of future practice.

Memory Room and Psychological Space presents the successful collaboration between the members of the collective *Carte Blanche*—a stage set (one of the rooms) designed for the play *I Love Todd Sampson*. The play is set across the floors of the Pier 2/3 at Walsh Bay in Sydney, with the memory room capturing the tangled psychological space of the play's central character Laura. There were eight other architectural teams (not always from the same practice) who designed and built the other rooms or sets for the other acts of the play. Carte Blanche also designed and installed Cloudscape, an interactive light installation at Sydney Harbour. *Communities in/of the Cloud* argues that this installation explored the notion of collective energy of people and networked nature of lives through the light installation that was activated only at the moment when a physical connection was made between people, and between people and the installation.

A more sophisticated responsive installation, Hylozoic Series by Philip Beesley for the Biennale of Sydney, is discussed in *In-animate*. Beesley's installation was part organic, part inorganic which moves, grows, and breathes responding to proximity, motion, and touch. Immersive environments are also created by interior geometries. *Immersive Space of Imagination* shows how architectural firm, LAVA creates continuous space out timber ribs, providing the space of imagination and fantasy within a restricted inner city plot. *Healing Colours and Geometries* shows how architectural firm Enter Projects transforms an existing office space of about 150 sq m by a non-linear shaping of the walls and the ceiling creating a space fit for healing for children with autism. LAVA and Enter Projects use innovation in digital design and fabrication in a purposeful manner. *Hovering Immaterially* and *Historical Imageries* highlights the popular public art in Sydney but above all it presents productive collaborations between artists, engineers and landscape designers; and artist and architects exploring also the relation between art, technology, identity, and the city.

4.2 Memory Room and Psychological Space

One of the big events to engage the imagination and interest of architectural practitioners, thinkers, journalists, and academic was the play by the Living Room Theatre titled I Love Todd Sampson directed by Michelle St Anne with Andy McDonald as the architectural producer. The play has been described by as a multidisciplinary work of theatre that integrates architecture, installation art, light, music, film and performance. Presented by *The Living Room Theatre*, it presents the story of a woman having reached middle age with the dissociative effects of an abusive past causing her to attach to

Figure 20 Memory Room [Photo: Tim da Rin]

objects rather than people. She slides towards suicide until one day Todd Sampson (television's advertising guru) comes into her life, and she fixates on him. Sampson himself is not involved in this project, though he has agreed to be filmed for one scene in the play (Architecture AU, 2013).

The play is set in Sydney's Walsh Bay Pier 2/3 in a series of rooms, which provide a set or a setting for the scenes of the play, such that performers as well as the audience move from one room to the next to witness the unfolding of the story. *Carte Blanche* was one of the eight architectural teams (Archival, Carter Williamson Architects, CKW, Sam Crawford Architects, Flatpac, Genevieve Lilley Architects, and WLTS, and *Carte Blanche*) that contributed to this event. *Carte Blanche* is a collective of Victoria Bolton, Nicole Chojecka, Caroline Comino, Kim Nguyen Ngoc and they designed the Memory Room in the play.

Figure 21 Memory Room [Photo: Tim da Rin]

In the play, the cellist occupies one end of the Memory Room with Laura in the other, as the performance plays out Laura's memories of the traumatic events experienced in the past. The room is, therefore, designed to evoke feelings of being enclosed yet unnerved, comforted yet smothered. Nguyen Ngoc explains that the Memory Room marks a point of departure from space as a representation and as an image to space as abstract. Carte Blanche experiments with psychological space—not always measurable and defined or even palpable as physical space. Kim Nguyen Ngoc, the founding member of Carte Blanche explains

The Memory Room is an abstract expressive installation. It uses the folds of a net as a metaphor for the mind struggling with traumatic memories and escaping dreams. The visual materiality of the net engages people on different levels of interpretations (Nguyen Ngoc, 2013).

It is useful to refer to the other rooms as a point of comparison to establish difference. Each architectural team adopts a unique approach and hence a spatial typology—Laura's Room is a hyper-real domestic space; the Kitchen is a pictorial space with furniture distorted to respond to perspectival foreshortening; the Motel Room is a collage/assemblage of found objects. In contrast the psychological space of the Memory Room is formless. It is a territory of entanglement between often contradictory but coexistent feelings such as happiness and depression. The use of fabric (hail mesh) to form interlinked and suspended canopy-like forms appropriately represents the sensation of being entangled in thoughts. At the same time without representing memory, the 'visual materiality' of the installations evokes interpretation and hence an active space of the psyche, rather than a mere setting for it (Nguyen Ngoc, 2013). The structure of the wharf was a determinant in the design and development of the Memory Room. It moves away from thinking of the room as a structure within a structure, towards thinking of the interior as emerging out of the interaction between the structure and installation. Nguyen Ngoc (2013) explains that even though the modelling of the room had been tested in 3D Max and Rhino, it really was shaped on site through a more hands-on process of self-installation.

Carte Blanche notes that the design of the set (setting) was an interesting project not because it was designed for the performance but that the performance itself grew out of the design of the set, thereby making the outcome truly collaborative. Their interest in temporary spaces is informed by the shorter turnaround time for materialization (as compared to buildings), providing an almost instant and tactile feedback. *Carte Blanche* thrives on collaborative relationships with clients. The purpose of coming together as a collective is to seek autonomy and alternative modes of expressions, to extend creative capacities and ambits of contribution. Loosely formed collectives (rather than more commercially centred notions of partnerships) in Sydney is an emerging mode of interdisciplinary practice. While *Carte Blanche's* work profile emerges as a response to emerging opportunities, it is also defined by its interest in crafting interactive connections between people.

4.3   Communities in/of the Cloud

Cloudscape, an interactive light architecture installation, was the key feature in the Vivid Sydney Festival 2012 (25 May to 11 June). Designed as a destination, a beacon, and a place to meet, the installation is a collaborative effort between Nicolas Thioulouse and Kim Nguyen Ngoc of Woods Bagot, and Michael Day, Frank Maguire, Victoria Bolton, Kristine Deray, with Woodsbagot, sponsored by Built, One Steel, Traxon e-cue, Inlite, Elan Construct, Enstruct, UTS. Situated at the Sydney Harbour, the installation is a grid covered with hundreds of inflatable silver mylar balloons. The designers explain that during the day, the balloons move with the wind and reflect the weather, transformed at night into an illuminated horizon and canopy. A pro bono installation (at the cost of 30,000 dollars, not including lights), Cloudscapes was a gift from Woods Bagot and the sponsors, intended to provoke curiosity and interaction amongst the visitors.

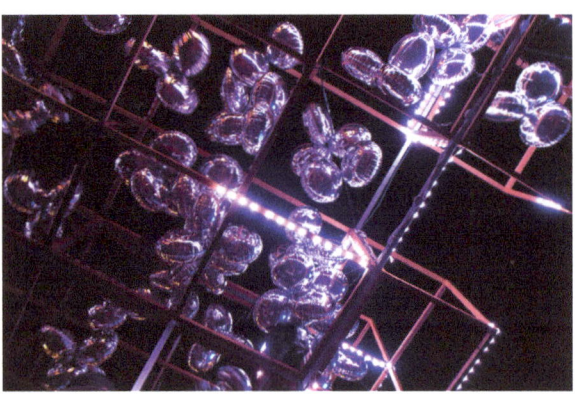

Figure 22 Cloudscape, Sydney Harbour, Vivid Sydney Festival 2012 [Photo: David Stefanoff]

Figure 23 Cloudscape, Sydney Harbour, Vivid Sydney Festival 2012 [Photo: David Stefanoff]

Cloudscape is an interesting term as it means that people 'act' as clouds 'casting' their shadows onto and over the silver balloons that constitute the light installation. They do so through interacting with the installation and with each other. A visitor's testimonial captures the experience: 'The best moment was when we saw people holding hands and forming a small chain under the installation to activate the lights. Then they were moving into a bigger and longer chain, about 30 people, kids and adults; it was a fantastic moment. Strangers holding hands and watching the clouds and the lights. A real moment of collective art (Nguyen Ngoc 2012).' The main thing was that it got strangers to interact with each other and hold hands for the briefest time. Cloudscape builds upon Alf (Artificial Light Form)—a light installation for Vivid Sydney 2011, designed by Kim Nguyen Ngoc, Victoria Bolton, Catherine Kuok, and Guy Hanson of Woodhead architects, along with Steven Brims of Umow Lai, Osram, Waterman, Philips Dynalite and Powersense. *Alf* was based on an interest in biodiversity and nature–city interactions, which 'led to the design of the artificial biomorphic entity that glows when people interact with it and sleeps with a subdued blue pulse when it is solitary (Globalhead, 2011).' The provocations for Cloudscape are similar yet different.

Thioulouse highlights the innate and primal desires of a human being, as he notes: 'As children we look for anthromorphic forms in the clouds; making sense of the universe by relating to our sense of self.' Similarly, Nguyen Ngoc calls upon 'our primal fears and fascination with clouds and thunderstorms,' which underpins the generation of 'storm of light effects' by the energy of people (Prince, 2012). The installation then is a response to these archaic human desires. However, Cloudscape is also a response to the manner in which identities and desires are construed in current times. As the contemporary person is a product of networked and connected thoughts, ideas, and people, Cloudscape fittingly evokes the metaphor of social media, as the direct and indirect alignments between people generate the energy to power the light effects. Nguyen Ngoc says: 'It creates the conditions for new and forgotten types of relationships between people, a sense of communion with climatic elements, by using electronic, photonic, and spatial constructions (Prince, 2012).' In doing so, Cloudscapes combines the natural, with the technological and the human—a symbol of our hybrid existence. This is what makes the installation meaningful, and not yet another light installation that is merely visually delightful, static, distant, and non-corporeal.

4.4 In-animate: Philip Beesley's Hylozoic Series: Sibyl

Canadian artist and architect Philip Beesley has contributed, to the 18th Biennale of Sydney 2012, the installation *Hylozoic Series: Sibyl*—an interactive, immersive, and sensory installation at Cockatoo Island. Beesley's work explores the thresholds between the animate and the inanimate, the natural and the artificial, and the intelligent and the mechanized, working across the disciplines of art and architecture. The installation is underpinned by the philosophy of Hylozoism. Beesley and Jonathan Tyrell explain Hylozoism as the 'ancient perception of life arising out of material…arising from the chaos–borne quickening of air, water, and stone. Implicit in this way of seeing the world is an oscillation and it might be said a certain ambiguity, between the parts and the whole. Out of this oscillation emerges a spirit that is not fully transcendent of its material origins and yet somehow distinct (Beesley and Tyrell, 2012, p. 379).

Figure 24 Hylozoic Series, Philip Beesley, Cockatoo Island, Sydney, The 18th Biennale of Sydney, 2012 [Photo: Anuradha Chatterjee]

Physically, the *Hylozoic Series* consists of 'hovering filter environments, composed of tiny laser cut acrylic elements,' 'groves of meshwork,' 'scented wicks and glands,' 'delicate glass spines,' 'seaweed-like filter clusters housing protocell flasks,' and 'gauze bladders' (Beesley, 2012). Caressing the glass spine makes it vibrate madly, which prompts the feathery wings to raise themselves. As we move on, the proximity sensors illuminate parts of the clusters in response to closeness and movement. Parts of the installation remain inert as they refuse to obey aggressive prompting. The balloon-like elements obviously expand and contract in response to the flow of people through the installation. Beesley and Rachel Armstrong (2011, p.83) also explain that the flasks and bladders contain protocells ('chemical models of primitive artificial cells'), which grow due to visitors' presence. These are imperceptible.

Figure 25 Hylozoic Series, Philip Beesley, Cockatoo Island, Sydney, The 18th Biennale of Sydney, 2012 [Photo: Anuradha Chatterjee]

In *Hylozoic Ground* (2010), Beesley explains: 'Akin to the functions of a living system, embedded machine intelligence allows human interaction to trigger breathing, caressing, and swallowing motions and hybrid metabolic exchanges (Beesley 2010a, p.13).' The composition is therefore a sensorial and charged environment of 'exquisitely deliberate weakness.' It is neither living nor inert, but somewhere in the middle (transitional). It is intended as an embodiment of collective or composite identity, emerging out of 'empathy, and perhaps even a space of desire, between the subject and its milieu (Beesley and Tyrell, 2012, p.380). This sets it apart from what is ordinarily understood as interactive installation, now a well-rehearsed genre.

While the *Hylozoic Series* makes a significant contribution to technical and poetic possibilities in the networked and multi-disciplinary fields of 'sustainable design, geotextiles, material science, environmental engineering, robotics, psychology, and biotechnology', it is somewhat alienating (Beesley 2010b). There is little chance on understanding the installation without 'surrendering' oneself fully to the language of the scholarship surrounding it. Also, the experience was not immersive. This was possibly because the visit to installation was closely managed, visitors told what they could touch and not touch, and told to follow the spatial split in the installation (one part responsive to touch, the other responsive to proximity and motion), thereby making it a disappointing experience and certainly incapable of producing what Beesley notes as the space of desire and empathic affinities. Ironically, the beauty of the installation too was overwhelming. The reliance on the familiar images of hybrid and multiple ecologies—skeletal, feathery, glandular, membranous, winged, mesh, grove like—is over-invested in formalism, and hence the visual. This undermined the accentuation of other senses.

Figure 26 Hylozoic Series, Philip Beesley, Cockatoo Island, Sydney, The 18th Biennale of Sydney, 2012 [Photo: Anuradha Chatterjee]

4.5 Healing Colours and Geometries: Edgecliff Medical Centre

Edgecliff Medical Centre for Autistic Children by Enter Projects—a project of such high social relevance—has been shortlisted for the 2013 Australian Interior Design Awards. Autismaus's report suggests that 'there is one child with an ASD on average in every 160 children in this age group which represents 10,625 children aged between 6 and 12 years with an ASD [Autism Spectrum Disorders] in Australia (Australian Advisory Board on Autism Spectrum Disorders).' At Edgecliff Medical Centre, the challenge was to deliver programmed spaces with atmosphere within an existing office space of about 150 sq m. Enter Projects is well-established in the field of digital design and fabrication, and the Medical Centre is yet another iteration of competently designed and digitally fabricated interiors. The priorities of the client were 'three radiating treatment rooms, a central reception area, lots of play spaces, soft furnishings like beanbags and excellent visibility (Enter Projects, 2012).' The rigid orthogonal space is dramatically transformed into another world through the use of non-linear geometries in three dimensions.

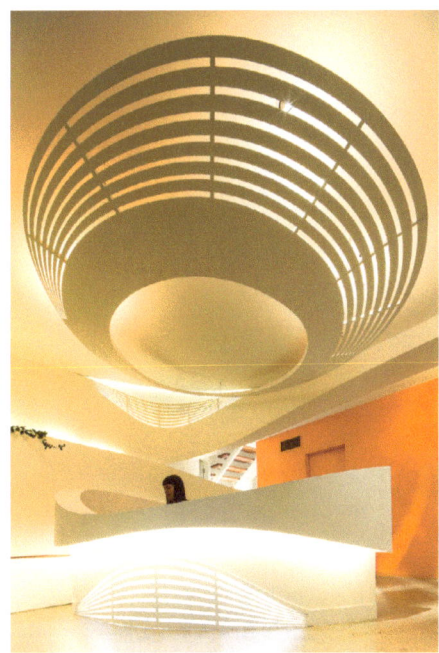

Figure 27 Edgecliff Medical Centre [Photo: Brett Boardman]

In 2010, Patrick Keane the director of Enter Projects curated an exhibition titled *From Form to Formless: Exploring Non-Linear Space for Five Decades* at Customs House in Sydney. It showcased rarely published and unpublished, local, built works by Hugh Buhrich, Stan Symonds, Reuben Lane, Harry Seidler and Associates, Durbach Block Jaggers Architects (in association with Peter Colquhoun), Enter Projects, Chris Bosse/LAVA, and the Airbus A380, presenting an undercurrent in Australian architectural practice that favours dynamic space and the use of non-orthogonal geometries. The exhibition celebrated the argument that space and occupants are in simultaneous and relative motion is concurrent with the use of non-orthogonal geometries in spatial organization, form (interior and exterior), and structure to achieve a fluid interaction between occupants and space. The Edgecliff Medical Centre for Autistic Children is clearly an exploration of this theme.

Figure 28 Edgecliff Medical Centre [Photo: Brett Boardman]

There are several environmental factors that need to be considered in designing interiors for children with autism. A.J. Paron-Wildes, an Industry Partner of American Society of Interior Designers through Allsteel and specializing in designing and advocating interior environments as places of healing with a focus on children with autism, argues that colour is significant. Paron-Wildes notes: 'Researchers have found that autistic children's rods and cones (components of the eye) have changed due to chemical imbalances or neural deficiencies. Of the autistic children tested, 85% saw colours with greater intensity than neurotypical children. For these children, red appears nearly fluorescent, vibrating with intensity (Paron-Wildes, 2012, p.2).' The second aspect that Paron-Wildes puts emphasis on is the clarity of layout. She notes: 'Neurologically challenged individuals often have difficulty following environmental cues. Many cannot distinguish normal visual cues such as exit or restroom signage. Yet careful attention to way finding and places of transition is crucial to their successful use of environments (p.2).'

The third aspect of interior design for children with autism is the removal of visual noise and clutter. Paron-Wildes explains that due to the 'occupant's savant skill of memorizing complex environments (i.e., all lines and shapes in an environment), existing shutters and drapery treatment… [would be] over-stimulating. Painting the window frame, and using the same colour shade [could create]…an intentionally uniform design' (p.2). The fourth aspect is lighting, which is capable of having a 'dramatic effect on people with neurological disorders, and special attention should be paid to glare, noise control, and flicker as these may be negative visual and audio stimuli (p.3).' Paron-Wildes recommends that electronic ballasts be used, as they 'greatly reduce flicker from fluorescent lamps,' along with locating 'ballasts high in the ceiling for better sound control,' and using uplighting or diffused lighting for reducing glare (p.3). Others like Christopher Beaver note the need for curved walls, corridor-less planning, and the designing of lighting to create a glow. Whilst these present a comprehensive set of guidelines for sensitive environmental design, the outcomes do not always possess character or inspiration. Such is not the case with Enter Projects' Edgecliff Medical Centre.

Enter Projects uses non-linear geometries not only to make the most of a restricted footprint but also to respond to the three most important aspects of the client's qualitative brief emerging out research into environments for autism—safety, visibility, and calmness. Most importantly, these qualities are brought into conversation rather than resolved independently. Enter Projects notes that the 'way in which the geometry circulates and unfolds not only promotes an atmosphere of calm, rest and relaxation but in severe circumstances, also prevents children from harming themselves on corners: where this space is concerned, right angles are most definitely the wrong angles (Enter Projects, 2012).' Furthermore, Patrick Keane the director of Enter Projects notes: 'The fluid nature of the space allows for good visibility and a playful quality. It is both intriguing and calming: no direct lights, no mechanical overstimulation to the senses. I always had Toyo Ito in the back of my mind and 'what not to do' based on the shopping centre across the street (Keane cited in Lynch, 2012).' Furthermore, the 'partnership of light, optics, and colour' is considered to as having a 'pivotal role in shaping the overall feel of the project. Indirect lighting was used to soften the space with cove lighting providing an additional calming effect (Enter Projects, 2012).'

Figure 29 Edgecliff Medical Centre [Photo: Brett Boardman]

The project is a success because it delivers an atmosphere, not just built space. This is achieved in the way the geometry of the interior informs and is co-informed by the layout, lighting, and furniture, to produce a whole with no distracting parts. The non-linear geometry structures the way finding through a corridor-less space made of curved walls. It consists of a gradual centrifugal circulation around the recognizable reception. The curved walls also provide a high level of visibility without necessarily having a panopticon effect. The non-linear geometry provides opportunities for built-in lighting and furniture, to reduce clutter and visual noise. The atmosphere is one of openness, connectedness, and a soft glow. Enter Projects has created a space of inspiration and innovation, by adapting the abstract design principle of dynamic space and non-orthogonal geometry to the meaningful design of a space of high social relevance and outcome.

4.6 Immersive Space of Imagination: LAVA's 'Other Worldly' Martian Embassy

The Martian Embassy designed by LAVA (Laboratory for Visionary Architecture, led by Chris Bosse) is the home of the Sydney Story Factory in Redfern Street, Sydney. Led by Catherine Keenan (co-founder and executive director), the 'Sydney Story Factory is a not-for-profit creative writing centre for young people in inner Sydney. Volunteer tutors help students to write and publish stories. Free programs target young people, from marginalized, Indigenous and non-English speaking backgrounds, but are open to everyone. It was inspired by 826 Valencia a creative writing centre for young people started by novelist Dave Eggers in San Francisco in 2002 (LAVA, 2012a).' The concept of the Martian Embassy is possibly informed by the flights of fancy that must underpin the act of transcending reality to enter the realm of imagination and fiction, where the encounter of the new, wonderful, and bizarre suggest endless possibilities.

Figure 30 Martian Embassy (View from the Embassy toward the Classroom) [Photo: Brett Boardman]

Largely a pro-bono project, the Martian Embassy was a collaboration between LAVA, Will O'Rourke (production), and The Glue Society (creative directors, and an independent creative collective located in Sydney and New York), who developed the Martian concept, involving also Berents

Project Management (Project Manager), ARUP (lighting and acoustic design), Redwood Projects (builder), Philips (lighting), Syntec (sound), and Avatar (oils). The kits of parts (both material and intellectual) donated generously by the project's multiple partners is stitched together effortlessly in the creation of an immersive interior that houses the Embassy, the Shop, and the Classroom.

The layout of the Martian Embassy is therefore akin to an 'intergalactic journey—from the embassy, at the street entrance, to the shop full of red planet traveller essentials, to the classroom. By the time kids reach the writing classes they have forgotten they are in "school" (LAVA, 2012b).' Constructed entirely out of CNC-cut plywood (1068 pieces), the interior consists of a system of repetitive spatial ribs that undulate in three dimensions to mould a fluid organic space. The spatial distinctions in the Martian Embassy are imperceptible, and the transitions between spaces are indicated subtly by the protrusion of fixed furniture and shelving, which are extensions of the skeletal system of the ribs. The skeletal ribs are not structural in the conventional sense of the word but they are spatio-structural. They structure or organize the occupation of the interior, highlighted also by the lines on the floor that continue on from the ribs. The three- and two-dimensional articulation of the fluid geometry prompts the body's rhythmic movement through space.

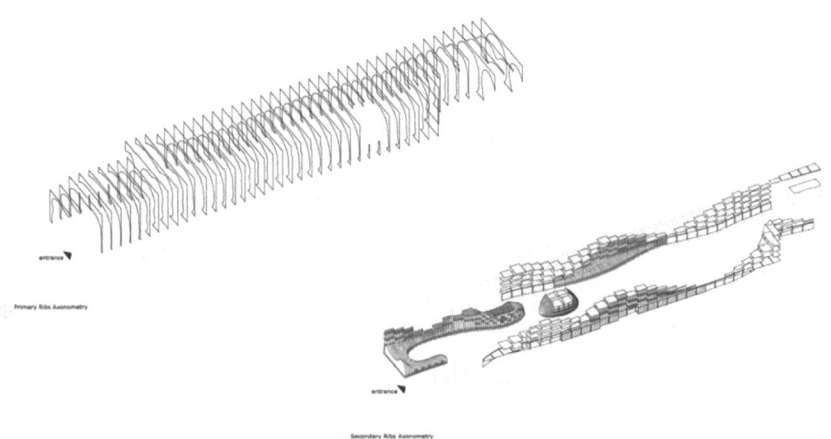

Figure 31 Martian Embassy, Primary Ribs and Secondary Ribs Axonometric, LAVA

The concept of fluid space makes the most of what could have been a narrow, deep, and dark space, devoid of daylight and dynamism. But at the Martian Embassy, the entry through the door in fact leads the eye through the interior to the sunlit backyard. The daylight filtering in is complemented by the changing LED light sequences that make different parts of the ribs glow in different colours at different times. It is as if the interiors were suffused with self-sustaining life. This demonstrates LAVA's interest in the synthesis of the organic and the technological. Hence, whilst they claim to derive the concept of the Martian Embassy from the 'fusion of a whale, a rocket, and a time tunnel,' they also admit indebtedness to the technologies from the 'yacht and space industry' in the creation of the timber ribs (LAVA, 2012b). The hybrid imagination of LAVA is clearly the perfect conduit for a creative writing centre. LAVA's expertise in working across scales, materials, typologies, and budgets (from the design of a lamp, a bookshelf, city planning, and towers) also informs the successful conceptualization and execution of the Martian Embassy.

Figure 32 Martian Embassy [Photo: Brett Boardman]

4.7 Hovering Immaterially: Halo in Chippendale Green, Central Park Sydney

Halo is a new public art designed as part of the Chippendale Green within Central Park, Sydney's new downtown destination. It is designed by artists Jennifer Turpin and Michaelie Crawford, in collaboration with specialist engineers, designers and fabricators lead by Jeremy Sparks of Partridge Event Engineering, and commissioned by Frasers Property Australia and

Figure 33 Halo, Halo Opening, 14 August 2012 [Photo: Anuradha Chatterjee]

Sekisui House Australia, the developers for Central Park. The work, notes Turpin, is an 'extraordinary integration of art, science, and engineering acting in collaboration with the natural environment (Central Park, 2013h).' Halo consists of a yellow ring (12 meters in diameter) attached to a sliver arm (6 meters long), aligned off centre and placed on top of a 13 metre high pole. Made of carbon fibre, the entire weight of the ring and the arm balances on a tiny ceramic bearing the size of a small glass marble. The ring moves with changing direction and gusts of wind. The artistic expression is indebted to the history of the site and the old brewery. Crawford notes that the 'beautiful circular supports for the enormous old brewing vats inspired Halo's form and a desire to reference the tipsy effects of beer resulted in the ring's precarious balance and off-centred tipping and turning (Central Park, 2013h).'

Figure 34 Halo, Halo Opening, 14 August 2012 [Photo: Anuradha Chatterjee]

Halo is interesting because whilst the concept is meaningful and its execution minimal and precise, it does nothing except demonstrate kinetic motion, but in doing little, it achieves a lot. Public art by its very nature is spatial, and its experiential dimension provides the programming of the public space it is placed within or against. *Halo* is placed at the end of the sloping path (and cascading water feature) that leads down to the Chippendale Green, designed by Danish landscape architect Jeppe Aagaard Andersen with Turf Design. *Halo* forms an imperceptible canopy connected to the trunk and firmly rooted to the ground. It provides also a scalar element to the space, which would otherwise be lost amidst the towers under construction. Like a canopy, it is ever present, seemingly protective, and moving with the breeze. It materializes the immaterial element—wind. It also frames the sky—not just as the figure of nature (cloudscapes) but also as the figure of the urban, through the framing of the rising towers around the Green.

Harriet F. Senie argues that 'the best time to write about public art is not when it is first installed but after it has "settled in,"' which would make this review a bit early (Senie, 2003). However, the public viewing of *Halo* on the 25 August 2012 (the Green formally opens in December 2012) demonstrated an enthusiastic public occupation. Installing a fragile environment and artefact (*Halo* and the Chippendale Green) within its harsher surrounds (construction of the towers) is perhaps an ironic but a sensible move. In this way, the public art and the space invited emotional and associational investments from the public, allowing it to become a part of local memory and identity. Halo provides an interpretation of the site and its history in its form but at the same time it provides an aperture and a conduit for the appreciation of the urban environment, and the reason to inhabit the surrounds.

4.8 Public Art in Sydney's Taylor Square: Historical Imageries

Located at Sydney's Taylor Square are two recently installed works of public art—the work of Aboriginal Australian artist Reko Rennie titled *Always Was Always Will Be*, and the work of British artist Tim Knowles, titled the *WindGrid*. These works are part of the City of Sydney's City Art Program, which seeks to enable artists to create public art that expresses and captures contemporary life while reflecting the unique history of Sydney, and in doing so create universally accessible experiences for the city's socially and culturally diverse communities. The aim is to 'embed public art into the fabric of the city' allowing for both permanent and temporary installations and artworks which 'reflect the changing ways artists and artworks engage with the life of the city, its communities and visitors (City of Sydney, no date, p.8). While the City of Sydney has a demonstrated interest in the care of statues, memorials and fountains within the boundaries of the local government area since the 1990s, the current program was developed and initiated in 2004. It has involved the integration of public art in new developments, community facilities, parks and street improvement programs (City of Sydney, no date).

The two works, both of which have been commissioned as temporary artworks, are located on either sides of Oxford Street—a busy arterial road that connects the city to the eastern suburb areas of Sydney. The works are strategically located at Taylor Square, which is a landmark location in Sydney. Formed in the early 1900s with the widening of Oxford Street by then Sydney Mayor, Allen Taylor (1864–1940), Taylor Square has historically been one of the busiest intersections in Sydney and has since undergone a series of redevelopment process in the late 1990s, and more recently in 2003 (Roberts, 1990). With its long-standing association with the city's nightlife, Taylor Square is perhaps best known as the venue of the Annual Gay and Lesbian Mardi Gras. Adding another layer of meaning to the social and cultural histories of the Square are the works of Rennie and Knowles.

Rennie belongs to the Kamilaroi or Gamilaraay people of north-western New South Wales. He employs art as a means of exploring 'issues of identity, race, law and justice, land rights, stolen generations and other issues affecting Aboriginal and Torres Strait Islanders in contemporary Australian society (Rennie, no date).' Drawing upon his Aboriginal ancestry and heritage, Rennie creates contemporary interpretations of traditional images through his artwork and installations using medium such as neon, projection, installation and spray paint. Through *Always Was Always Will Be*, Rennie alludes to the Gadigal people who were (and are still acknowledged as) the traditional owners of the land, in and around Sydney. The artwork comprises of geometric diamond patterns painted in bright fluorescent colours across the facades of the heritage listed former Commonwealth Bank, with the words *Always Was Always Will Be* in large neon text attached to the front façade of the building. The geometric diamond patterns draw upon Rennie's 'associations to north-western NSW and the traditional markings of the Kamilaroi people (Rennie, no date).' The artwork therefore represents a layering of Aboriginal and non-Aboriginal/European heritage(s) as it refers to the pre-colonial Aboriginal past, the colonial white Australian past and the current interpretation of Aboriginal presence in the city.

The WindGrid (previously) situated on the opposite, northern side of Taylor Square comprises of a series of paper aeroplanes stretched over a wire grid, suspended as a 'constantly shifting ceiling' over Taylor Square (City of Sydney, 2012b). Knowles indicates that the WindGrid was inspired by his previous works that featured 'wind as an invisible force; something beyond our control. It can be used, but neither captured nor contained (City of Sydney, 2012c).' He has deliberately used tiny aeroplanes as these are 'easily recognisable, universally familiar objects,' which audiences can identify with more readily, than with abstract or graphic shapes (City of Sydney, 2012c). The aim was to create a series of wind vanes, which could capture people's attention and make them observe the changing wind patterns as they move through or in and out of Taylor Square. Through this work, Knowles sought to present a different view to the public—a view that is based on 'the idea of harmony with nature; having a light touch, not leaving a trace.' The wind vanes reflect this temporariness in terms of movement with the wind, casting shadows on the paving of the Square, and by the very nature of the project. It is a temporary artwork that is to be replaced by Knowles' other tie-in projects—*WindLab* and *WindWalks* (City of Sydney, 2012c).

The artworks are considerably different in fulfilling the objectives of the City Art Program, as Rennie's work presents a layering of history(s) whereas Knowles connects to the idea of making the artwork more accessible to a wider audience. However the two artists are very similar in their aim of presenting the very aspects of either history and tradition (in the case of Rennie) or nature (in the case of Knowles) that are not immediately apparent or visible to the public, and in doing so they both submit to the temporary nature of their artworks and require an active engagement by the onlooker.

References

ArchitectureAU: Architecture, Interiors and Landscape (2013). 'I Love Todd Sampson: Voices of the Vulnerable.' Available from: http://architectureau.com/calendar/public-event/i-love-todd-sampson-voices-of-the-vulnerable/. [Accessed 09 May 2014].

Australian Advisory Board on Autism Spectrum Disorders. The Prevalence of Autism in Australia Can it be Established from Existing Data? Available from: http://autismaus.com.au/uploads/pdfs/PrevalenceReport.pdf [Accessed 09 March 2014].

Beesley P. (2010a). *Hylozoic Ground: Liminal Responsive Architecture*. Eds Hayley Isaacs and Pernilla Ohrstedt. Riverside Architectural Press Toronto, Ontario.

Beesley P. (2010b). Canadian Pavilion Venice Biennale 2010: Hylozoic Ground. Available from: http://www.hylozoicground.com/Venice [Accessed 09 March 2014].

Beesley P. and Armstrong R. (2011). 'Soil and Protoplasm: The Hylozoic Ground Project.' *Architectural Design: Protocell Architecture*, 81, 2, 78–89.

Beesley P. (2012). Hylozoic Series: Sibyl. http://www.philipbeesleyarchitect.com/sculptures/1036_Sibyl/index.php

Beesley P. and Tyrell J. (2012). Transitional Fields: Empathy and Affinity, in de Zegher C. and McMaster G., *The 18th Biennale of Sydney: All Our Relations*, Sydney, The 18th Biennale of Sydney, 379–381.

Central Park (2013h). Halo. Available from: http://www.centralparksydney.com/halo [Accessed 15 July 2013].

City of Sydney (n.d.). City Art: Public Art Strategy. Available from: http://www.cityartsydney.com.au/cityart/documents/FinalVersionCityArtPubilcArtStrategy.pdf [Accessed 09 May 2014].

City of Sydney (2012b). Taylor Square Art: Windgrid. Available from: http://www.artandabout.com.au/events/windgrid/ [Accessed 9 May 2013].

City of Sydney (2012c). Wind Talk with Tim Knowles. Available from: http://www.cityartsydney.com.au/cityart/news/?cat=36 [Accessed 9 May 2014].

Enter Projects (2012). Edgecliff Medical Centre Text.

Globalhead (2011). 'Artificial Light Form.' Globalhead WordPress. Available from: https://globalhead.wordpress.com/2011/07/04/alf/. [Accessed 09 May 2014].

LAVA (2012a). Press Release: The Martians have Landed, 20 July.

LAVA (2012b). Martian Embassy. Available from: http://www.l-a-v-a.net/projects/martian-embassy [Accessed 09 March 2014].

Lynch O. (2012). 'Edgecliff Medical by Enter Projects,' IndesignLive. Available from: http://www.indesignlive.com/parties/article-gallery/Edgecliff-Medical-Centre-by-Enter-Projects [Accessed 09 March 2014].

Nguyen Ngoc, K. (2013). Interview, 20 February.

Nguyen Ngoc, K. (2012). Visitor Testimonial for Cloudscapes.

Prince M. (2012). 'Woods Bagot Creates Art Installation for Vivid Sydney.' Architecture and Design, 16 May. Available from: http://www.architectureanddesign.com.au/news/industry-news/woods-bagot-creates-art-installation-for-vivid-syd [Accessed 09 March 2014].

Paron-Wildes A.J., 'Sensory Stimulation and Autistic Children,' *Implications: A Newsletter by InformeDesign*, 6, 4. Available from: http://www.informedesign.org/_news/apr_v06r-pr.pdf [Accessed 09 March 2014].

Roberts A. (1990). 'Taylor, Sir Allen Arthur (1864–1940),' *Australian Dictionary of Biography*, National Centre of Biography, Australian National University. Available from: http://adb.anu.edu.au/biography/taylor-sir-allen-arthur-8753/text15335 [Accessed 9 May 2014].

Rennie R. (nd). Reko Rennie. Available from: http://www.rekorennie.com/index.php [Accessed 9 May 2014].

Senie H.F. (2003). 'Responsible Criticism: Evaluating Public Art,' *Sculpture: A publication of the International Sculpture Center*, 22, 10. Available from: http://www.sculpture.org/documents/scmag03/dec03/senie/senie.shtml [Accessed 15 July 2013].

Chapter 05

Ideas: Sites, Sights, and Visions

Abstract: In Sydney, architectural practice is at large dominated by well-rehearsed and pragmatic concerns with sustainability, housing, redevelopment and urban renewal, with little challenge to the inclusions and exclusions that form the foundations of these institutions and their discourses. New ways of looking at social ethics, authorship, narrative, agency, as users and designers is important to keep architecture critical of its own limits and objectives. The inventions take on a diffuse and dispersed form, as studios, urban projects, collectives, exhibitions, PhD theses, and so on.

Key words: Collaborative practices, gender and work, projective mapping

5.1 Introduction

In Sydney, architectural practice is at large dominated by well-rehearsed and pragmatic concerns with sustainability, housing, redevelopment and urban renewal, with little challenge to the inclusions and exclusions that form the foundations of these institutions and their discourses. New ways of looking at social ethics, authorship, narrative, agency, as users and designers is important to keep architecture critical of its own limits and objectives. These inventions and re-inventions take on a diffuse and dispersed form, as studios, urban projects, collectives, exhibitions, PhD theses, and so on.

The chapter *N: Speaking in Different Voices* presents an interdisciplinary curatorial collective, comprising of people who operate across and at the threshold of art, architecture, performance, and media, are now separated by distance of continents, and who use their individual creative practices to collaborate find projects and forums that lend themselves to socio-political purpose and the opportunity for experimental works. *Women and the Other Domains of Architectural Production* responds to the launch of Archiparlour, which very broadly speaking, focuses on the absence or a discontinuous presence of women in the profession of architecture or at higher positions. I suggest here that we also make visible the ongoing contributions made by women in the other aspects of the profession, which may not be properly considered a form of practice, suggesting the need to reinvent the definition of the word profession or professional in architecture, to include a different modes and agencies of contributions. *Spatial Narratives and Deviant Conditions* continues the redefinition of terms as it looks into a recording of site and territory as a creative act of projective mapping. It presents the work currently being developed by Tom Rivard, a Sydney-based academic, which challenges the historical concept of space as measurable, and a tradable commodity as real estate and property.

Imagining other Cities continues the discussions on territory, as it challenges the boundaries between city and the suburb, with the suburb seen now as the unsustainable and underperforming wasteland of little value. Driven by the initiative of governmental and non-governmental actors, Super Sydney aimed to discover the urbanism of suburbs, which remain unacknowledged and untapped. The people of Sydney imagine individually as well as collectively their urban utopias, shifting the emphasis away from the economy of scale dominated by corporate investment to one that is authentically located in place, shared cultures, and memory. The role of the user at the scale of house is considered in *Rural Habitat* through the work of Mobile Workshop Architects (MWA) from Mexico who demand equality for users, especially when they are already at a financial disadvantage. Designing for rural populations, MWA propose an altered professional ethic: build like you would build for yourself and like you would live in it, while also taking into account cultural desires and needs of the people.

5.2   N: Speaking in Different Voices

N is an interdisciplinary curatorial collective founded in 2010 by Sam Spurr, Adrian Lahoud, and David Burns, and recently it has been increasingly visible in leading discussions concerning the intersections between architecture and urbanism with visual and performance arts. Spurr, Lahoud, and Burns are/were academics at the University of Technology Sydney. The interdisciplinarity of the cohort is thus made possible: Spurr is a designer and theorist with interest in performance; Lahoud is an urbanist; and Burns is interested in images and installations. N is therefore interested in the links as well as the gaps between art and architecture, positioned against issues pertaining to the city. Furthermore, the curation is not of objects but of ideas and conversations that are as material as built works. They note in their website the different typologies of conversations as 'adversarial,' 'roundtable,' 'radial,' 'lecture,' 'linear,' and 'studio,' declaring their commitment as follows: 'N's research involves the study of the typologies of conversation and their impact on art, architecture, and design' (N, no date a). Hence, the projects undertaken by N have almost always involved the organization of panel discussions, roundtables, and interviews and talks with and between designers, commentators, and philosophers. Above all, they are interested in creating 'non-institutional spaces for practice, knowledge and social action through events and forums related to art and architecture (N, no date a).'

How to be a Good Witness is the architecture section of the 2011 Prague Quadrennial. It explored the productivity of the gap between linguistic practices of interpreting and translating through a range of exhibited works surrounding the concept mapping of the city. Gwangju Design Biennale Networks of Surrender 2011 (also curated by Nicole Bearman) highlighted the potency of sharing, blurring of ideas and words as they 'transform the image of this harbour city from generic postcard perfection to a set of multiplicitous, individual urban narratives' (N, no date b). INDEX Forum 2011 involved Charles Renfro of Diller Scofidio + Renfro, New York and Eva Franch I Gilabert of the Storefront for Art and Architecture in New York. It was a roundtable conversation on the way cultural events can change a city (N, no date c). N collaborated with Kaldor Public Art Projects on a series of events to coincide with the *The Dailies* by German artists Thomas Demand, which attempted to 'capture everyday moments and objects (Kaldor Art Projects, 2012).' N organized *The Doppelgänger* Parlour and *The Mirror Parlour* events, which included panel discussions, model-making workshops, architectural interventions, and film screenings (N, no date d). More recently, N was commissioned by the Office for Good Design in Melbourne to conduct interviews with local and international designers to explore the connection between design, happiness, community, belonging, and civic well-being (Office for Good Design, 2012). N also directed the Audio Architecture (curated by Office for Good Design). Exploring a spatial study of dissonance, the students explored the creative and collaborative intersections of sound and architecture through workshops, discussions, performances, and design experiments. The provocation was to create a space in tension, oscillating between harmony and discord, an analysis centering on states of instability and their inherent dynamism (N, no date e).

What is really interesting about N is their commitment to conversations rather than objects. As academics and architects/designers, the collaborators undertake a research-practice of a different kind. Burns notes that their sister organization is the Office for Good Design and New York based AND ANDAND. At least in Sydney, this is as yet an unrecognizable form of practice as it is not predicated by known and codified formal and curatorial strategies and outcomes. The interdisciplinary collective of Spurr, Lahoud, and Burns informs N's interest in the notions of the untranslatable gaps between language and form, and intellectual space as a shared realm. Of course, N is conscious of building models of engagement that involve wider disciplinary participation. However, what is most intriguing is the migratory and elusive nature of these engagements and contributions, hence making the whole collective rather unpredictable, which is a positive thing.

5.3 Women and the Other Domains of Architectural Production

The launch of Parlour: Women, Equity, Architecture, an outcome of the Parlour, is an outcome of the Australian Research Council funded project titled Equity and Diversity in the Australian Architecture Profession: Women, Work, and Leadership, led by Dr Naomi Stead, Dr Karen Burns, Professor Julie Willis, Justine Clark, Professor Sandra Kaji-O'Grady, Gill Matthewson, Dr Amanda Roan, Professor Gillian Whitehouse and Professor Susan Savage (Clark et al., 2014). As the forum 'seeks to expand the spaces and opportunities available to women while also revealing the many women who already contribute in diverse ways,' it got me thinking not just of equity, opportunity, and visibility of women in architectural practice, but also of women's contribution to the broader discourse of architecture or the way in which gender could reconceptualise or expand the boundaries of the profession (Clark et al.,

2014). As a scholar in architectural humanities, I consider the term as a wider field of curating, writing, managing, and marketing architecture. Taking a documentary strategy as opposed to historiographical one, I mapped the lived experience of my interactions and collaborations with women in leadership positions in Sydney for over a period of six months, in these other domains of architectural production.

From the middle of year, the Australian Architecture Association planned the four-part talk series titled *Women Take on Design* that featured Archrival (Claire McCaughan and Lucy Humphrey), Caroline Pidcock, Heather Whitely-Robertson, and Annalisa Capurro. The talk series was as interesting as it was successful. It should be mentioned that Australian Architecture Association, which 'supports discourse and the promotion of architecture in the Australian cultural milieu,' is activated by the energetic leadership of Annette Dearing as the Founding Director, and Vanessa Couzens as the Volunteer, Architect, Designer, Project Manager, and Editor (Australian Architecture Association, 2014). The Sydney Architecture Festival brought forth the women in the public life of architecture. The festival was organized, managed, delivered, and marketed by Siobhan Abdurahman (Projects Officer, NSW Architects Registration Board) and Gillian Redman-Lloyd (Events & Marketing, NSW Architecture Awards Manager). The range of talks, tours, exhibitions, and workshops aimed to engage the many interests and capacities of its collaborators and audiences.

Jennifer Kwok (Manager, Customs House Sydney) is not an architect. She is a designer by training and a perceptive thinker in the architectural, urban, digital, and virtual realities. She has produced many architecture exhibitions such as *Form to Formless, Remodelling Architecture, Transclimatic* to name just a few, and her creative direction and acumen in production was instrumental in my curatorial contribution to Inter-action, the Sydney Architecture Festival exhibition consisting of six independent exhibits. Along similar lines, my collaboration with Ann Quinlan (Program Director for Architecture from 2010 to 2012, Faculty of Built Environment, UNSW) also informed the curation of BE X Section, also a Sydney Architecture Festival exhibition. Quinlan has been instrumental in quietly but astutely providing directorial and curatorial advice and direction to many exhibitions in the Faculty, otherwise a well-respected scholar in the field of architectural education and pedagogy.

Other key contributors to the Sydney Architecture Festival included Joni Taylor, a researcher, writer, and curator focusing on the transformation of the urban environment, curated *The Third Landscape* at the Tin Sheds Gallery. Taylor explains:

The exhibition examines the transformative possibilities for regenerating seemingly negative landscapes of the forgotten and the blighted. Taking French gardener Gilles Clément's term for nature's reclamation of wasteland as its title, it presents artists, architects and designers whose work addresses the adaptability of interstitial spaces. These works demonstrate not only how spontaneous biodiversity can occur in these spaces, but diverse social and cultural activities too (Taylor, 2012).

As part of the Festival, Annette Mauer, Head of Learning at the Object Gallery, organised a workshop called *Building Connections*, for teachers and students at the Museum of Contemporary Arts Australia. In an email message on 26 November 2012, Mauer explained: 'The aim of both the workshop and resource was to make architecture accessible to visual arts teachers and relevant to their teaching the Visual Arts syllabus. The workshop was a great success with an exchange of ideas and information as well as a practical activity. The teachers and students had an opportunity to work with practising architects.'

Dearing and Couzens made a substantial contribution to the Festival by organizing the talk by Ken Yeang as well as the planned walks around key public domains in Sydney. Other contributors to the Festival included Aanya Roennfeldt (Gallery Curator, DAB LAB, UTS), who contributed curatorial insights to William Feuerman's exhibition and talk titled The Mechanics of Visual Perception, and Imogene Tudor, whose co-directorial role in Make Space for Architecture would have been vital to the success of the event, *Public Space: Private Interest*. Unrelated to the Sydney Architecture Festival but coincident with it was the launch of Kylie Legge's book *Doing it Differently*, a well-timed publication on urban living and city making, focusing on collaborative consumption (a concept made popular by *What's Mine is Yours* by Rachel Botsman and Roo Rogers).

This piece, which I am sure is full of omissions, suggests the possibility of a more inclusive sociology of practice, which will allow for the expansion of the definition of architectural practice, beyond what is legitimized by the legal status of the architect, such that the other *stuff that women* do can become included in the *business of architecture*. That this is a timely argument is evidenced by the talk recently organized at Tusculum, home of the Australian Institute of Architects, NSW Chapter. The talk was titled What's your Architecture, the Multifaceted Career Path that is an Architecture Degree The Photographer; the Journo; the Artists; the Builder, and it featured Brett Boardman (Architecture + photography), Michael Lewarne and Tom Rivard (Architecture + art), David Neustein (Architecture and Journalism), and Drew Heath (Architecture + building), failing to once again acknowledge women's contributions in this area. This piece itself is imperfect because it does not as yet include women in complementary disciplines of photography, teaching, animation, illustration, graphic design, performance, set design, and so on. Perhaps when the picture is complete, we may even discover fuller participation of women in what we call architectural practice.

5.4 Spatial Narratives and Deviant Conditions

Arcade 4 / Points of Departure: Migratory Evidence (753 BC to 2018 AD) was a collaborative exhibition at Gaffa Gallery in Sydney, curated and produced by Tom Rivard, a curator, architect, artist, and researcher with University of Technology Sydney Interior Spatial students (Alecia Downie, Heather Ho, Natalie Rumore, Arwen Sachinwalla, and Olivia Savio-Matev). The exhibition takes the World Heritage Listed Cockatoo Island, one of the Sydney's largest islands, as its site and subject. The island, which houses many annual events like the Biennale of Sydney, is a perfect non-place in the urban imaginary of many architectural thinkers in Sydney, and has stimulated many urban speculations and studios such as Urban Islands. The exhibition is one of the projects that will contribute to Rivard's PhD dissertation, which 'explores a projective mapping that affords the incorporation of disparate applied narratives, the derivation of spatial projects, and the establishment of a new measure of the world, both real and fictive (Rivard, 2013a).'

Figure 35 Tom Rivard, Table of Contents, *Arcade 4 / Points of Departure: Migratory Evidence* 753 BC to 2018 AD

The notion of 'projective mapping' is interesting because it is a representation of real and unreal, past and future, palpable and the intangible, physical and the ethereal, meaningful and the trivial, individual and the collective (Rivard, 2013a). However, above all it is the means through which personal narratives and interpretations can be inscribed into and as a map to then intuit urban opportunities, hence projects of greater meaning. The reference to 'a new measure of the world' is also interesting because it exceeds the finite ambit of cartographic representation (Rivard, 2013a). As a result, the exhibits are representational hybrids. The exhibits are: Table of Contents, Portraits and accompanying *Sections*, and *Evidence* on plinths in the exhibition space. The *Table of Contents* and the *Portraits* are simultaneously a map, tracing, painting, relief model, and even oddly, satellite images of remote sensing archaeology. The *Evidence* are machines and art—non-functional hybrids. The *Sections* are vignettes, dioramas, and models. Furthermore, the act of drawing is also an act of *drawing out*, such that architectural representation is a performative and active presenting of reality previous unknown to the eye and the mind. The map, only momentarily, provides the instrumentation of the 'cartographic method of triangulation,' in the case of locating the site for one of the ramps (Rivard, 2013b). Projective mapping is also concerned with drawing out the pre-history of the site, which has mystical allusions that challenge the empirical vision of the historian/surveyor. The allusion to the new measure of space is also a contemporary challenge to a historical concept of space as measurable, and hence a tradable commodity as real estate and property.

Figure 36 Alecia Downie, Theseus, *Arcade 4 / Points of Departure: Migratory Evidence 753 BC to 2018 AD*

Figure 37 Tom Rivard, Section, Floating Theatre, *Arcade 4 / Points of Departure: Migratory Evidence 753 BC to 2018 AD*

The exhibition focuses on the gap, break, fissure, or the threshold between things. Rivard is interested in 'liquid history' as it attends to an interest in the thresholds in water (or watery thresholds) such as ocean pools and the associated conditions of slippage, such that the boundaries are thresholds that do not begin or end, but are always in condition of making, remaking, and unmaking (Rivard, 2013b). In this form, the threshold is non-territorial, and it challenges the fixed ideas of ownership of public domain. Along these lines, Rivard locates the premise of the exhibition as

> The space between what things seem and what they are is the territory. The greater the terrain we construct in this gap, the more room we have to wander, unconstrained by either physical conditions or programmatic demands. Like Daedalus' Labyrinth, this terrain contains within it the real and the unreal, the past as well as the future. As a fragmentation of time and space, the results posit a disjointed geography of excisions and allegory; importantly, one wide open to interpretation (Rivard, 2013a).

Fittingly, then the exhibition focuses on the theme of migration, which attends to the migratory processes of matter leaving and entering the island through ebbs and flows of natural and occupational forces, which erodes as well as deposits to make these territories. The gap between sense and non sense, leaving and arriving, reading and not comprehending is the space that is being referred to as the space of immense potential. Rivard is interested in what he terms as the 'deviant condition or deviant threshold'—the space in between things, which can be occupied but cannot be tamed and conquered (Rivard, 2013b).

Rivard and his student collaborators Downie, Ho, Rumore, Sachinwalla, and Savio-Matev occupy this gap/threshold in knowledge and authorship. The student collaborators are encouraged to invent and uncover 'narratives about incongruous objects' found on site (Rivard, 2013b). Each collaborator works with a set of parameters, which include an archetype (figures from Greek mythology such as Theseus, Phaedra, Pasiphae, Ariadne, and Minotaur), sense, situation, operation, reaction, accompany (music), and migratory program. Arwen Sachinwalla explores the conditions as follows:

Ariadne – The goddess of nature & culture; abandoned and future bride. Woman

Sense – Touch

Situation – The Dog Leg Tunnel, connecting the Eastern Apron with the Southern Precinct, where everyone on the Island took refuge when the Japanese midget submarines shelled Sydney Harbour in 1942.

Operation – Two borings meet unexpectedly.

Reaction – Containment

Accompany – Leonard Cohen, Avalanche

Migratory Program – Map Room – traces

(Beyond floating terrain, water within water comes to land) (Rivard, 2013a)

This triggers the Portraits produced by Rivard—the first 'narrative overlay' of the 'deep mythology' of Cockatoo. Rivard explains that these discoveries are 'mapped back onto the Island (via the *Table of Contents*), by triangulating the sites with threshold conditions, exhibiting an affinity to the archetypes and sites,' which then inform and prompt the next set of projects (Rivard, 2013a). Here the second 'narrative overlay' of 'migratory projections' is enacted (Rivard, 2013a). For Rivard, this materializes into Sections and for the students, Evidence. For instance, the *Portrait* for the archetype of Theseus by Alecia Downie generates the *Weather Machine*, and Rivard's *Section*, the Aquatic Theatre. The Sections are experientially rich spaces that engage multiple senses of touch, vision, taste, hearing, and smell. They highlight, display, perform, exacerbate, and celebrate the found and created conditions on Cockatoo Island.

The interaction of different modes of discovery, mapping, and making are somewhat chemical, and hence deviant, not only in terms of the representation but also authorially. The authorship is blurred not as a designed outcome of the exhibition's curation. It is the unavoidable result of the untranslatable gaps in knowledge, intention, and direction between Rivard and his collaborators that resonates the focus on deviant thresholds and liquid histories. As the authorship of the work never declares its end and the other's beginning, it is truly a spin on the corporate notion of collaboration, in the sense that Arcade 4 performs and hence discovers the chemistries of collaboration rather than playing out a pre-given itinerary of action and agency.

5.5   Imagining Other Cities: Super Sydney

Super Sydney, a project launched by architects Tim Williams and Andrew Burns, examines metropolitan challenges for city by inviting, collating, and interpreting the visions and aspirations of many communities by conducting video interviews in each of the forty one local councils in Sydney. The organizers note: 'Through the democratization of Sydney's voice, we will build a Metropolitan consciousness (Super Sydney, 2012).' The findings and collated video interviews were presented at the Sydney Architecture Festival in October. The process of hearing, understanding, and re-telling hundreds of individual narratives aims to build metropolitan consciousness and relevance as well as reveal the wealth of knowledge that is contained in the imagination of the citizens at large. A few things than can be said about the events and ideas surrounding this project are as follows.

The first point is the variety and the number of people who are involved in the project. In addition to the working group, which included Sydney architects Tim Williams, Andrew Burns and Adam Russell, as well as Eva Rodriguez-Riestra, Gillian Redman-Lloyd from the Australian Institute of Architects and Penny Craswell, Editor of *Artichoke* magazine, there were many volunteer interviewers (architects and designers from all over Sydney) who are conducting these video interviews, not to mention the Council members. In addition, the interviewers were assisted by about 40 architecture students from the Masters studio at the University of Sydney (Coordinator: Lee Stickells with tutors Anuradha Chatterjee, Tom Rivard, and Tim Williams). This made Super Sydney firstly (and lastly) a collaborative and collective undertaking.

The second point is the speculative dimension to this project. Historically, studio projects (in addition to schemes for design competition and other unbuilt projects) have been the experimental ground for imagining urban possibilities. University of Sydney architecture students engaged with this by focusing on ten councils, to discern specific opportunities and challenges for housing, working, cultural experience, sustainability and transport. Students were expected to synthesize these directions with the findings from the video interviews to present proposals for urban initiatives. The initiatives could be built or unbuilt in the sense that they could include community markets, new infrastructures, bridges and crossings, urban farms, new transport networks, virtual communities, affordable housing, programming parks for inclusive use, foreshore revitalizations, temporal and pop up urbanism, and so on.

The third point is that the focus on the suburban domains as opposed to the City and inner City is long overdue, refreshing, and well-timed. Not only was Super Sydney informed by the success of *The Future of Penrith, Penrith of the Future* and the union of Councils in Paris called *Paris Métropole* (also involving Tim Williams), but it was also coincident with trends in the United States. Ellen Dunham Jones has become popular for book *Retrofitting Suburbia*. She advocates densifying as well as adapting to new uses those areas that are severely underperforming. Dunham Jones discusses the need to redirect lot more of our growth into existing communities, build up and re-inhabitation of underused parking lots, and adaptation of dead malls as universities, nursing homes and so on. International Making Cities Liveable Conference also announced a similar premise with invitations to exhibit: Successful Designs for Reshaping Suburbia.

In Sydney, not only there is the real need to think along these lines (now that we have somewhat come to terms with the full extent of urban sprawl and lifeless suburban landscapes that promise no optimism or opportunity for public life), but there is a real opportunity. Each council area is marked by complex history, topography, cultural mix, geographical boundaries, and proximities, revealing issues and concerns that demand urban intervention, repair, or augmentation. It is this innate, endemic, and located opportunities for urbanism that Super Sydney aims to tease out. The lasting influence of Super Sydney, I suspect, will also be in providing a revised context for judging merit of architectural merit—as the sophisticated and thoughtful articulation of broader urban aims, and not mere formal and technological sophistry, or banal programmatic delivery.

5.6   Rural Habitat

Rural Habitat, an exhibition of low-cost housing for rural and remote communities in Mexico by Mobile Workshop Architects (MWA) in collaboration with NGO Vasco de Quiroga PXXI, opened in Customs House, for the Sydney Architecture Festival. Mobile Workshop Architects is led by Isaac and Jacob Smeke, young Mexican architects, based in Sydney and Mexico. On exhibition is one prototype and one dwelling for the Trinidad family (Don Gregorio and Nicolasa and their eight kids). MWA see architecture as helping with life: not just shelter but also health and social life (Smeke and Smeke, 2013a). It is not just the physical requirements that have to be met, but also people's need to organize themselves into communities, have better health and well-being, and generate wealth that need to be addressed. If architecture provides only the physical fabric, it would have failed. Therefore, MWA's practice also involves the delivery of social and technological projects. These projects are occasions to harness existing and develop new skills and products, and market and commercialize them. In terms of the social projects, MWA are interested in projects like 'Patrullitas Ecologicas (environmental patrols)'. MWA explain that the project encourages children to get involved in recycling and generating natural fertilisers for community farming projects. Children across a range of towns can assist in the collection of Polyethylene terephthalate or PET bottles which are used to store organic waste which is then deposited into earthworm tanks. The compost generated creates rich fertilizer which can be recycled into local gardens and farms or sold on. When the bottles have been emptied, they can be sold to PET bottle collectors. Money generated from this after-school project contributes directly to school excursions but more importantly teaches children the importance of regenerative environmental projects (Smeke and Smeke, 2013b).

Figure 38 Biomass Stove, Trinidad Family House (Don Gregorio and Nicolasa), by Mobile Workshop Architects

In terms of the technological projects, MWA leads the design of the Biomass stove, which not only benefits the health of women, but it also reduces non-sustainable logging and emission of greenhouse gases. They explain that the

> Burning at up to 480°Celsius the newer [biomass] stove design produces and preserves heat more effectively than previous 'Patsari' stove designs which have required 90% more timber to run. Foraged branches rather than timber logs sufficiently fuel this stove, which includes a flue to extract smoke away from its user. Reduced smoke inhalation makes this stove a significantly healthier version than other out-dated stoves (Smeke and Smeke, 2013b).

These projects are not merely *home-delivered*. Communities are enabled to apply for and utilize grants from the government through active participation in the project and collaboration with other members of the community, based on the principles of social mortgage along the lines of that advocated by Professor Muhammad Yunus (Smeke and Smeke, 2013a).

Figure 39 Exterior, Trinidad Family House (Don Gregorio and Nicolasa), by Mobile Workshop Architects

While all this is noble and relevant, the field of *architecture for humanity* is actually a long-standing stream of architectural practice as NGOs and architects have worked collaboratively for decades in many fragile communities. So what is different about these projects? First, Isaac and Jacob overtly adopt a moral position, indicating an ownership of these projects. They are not mere facilitators: they are authentically invested in what they build. They ask: 'How can you tell people how to live? And, how can you design something you would not live in yourself?' (Smeke and Smeke, 2013b) They note: '[N]ot because some people are less fortunate economically or culturally different we have to see them as second class citizens or impose a westernized idea on how to live but rather celebrate their cultural inheritance and their way of life by learning from their experience (Smeke and Smeke, 2013b).' These questions are confronting. They allude to the discrepancies between design standards and the realities of occupancy, especially exacerbated in the projects for the rural or the urban poor. The expert knowledge upon which the profession of architecture is legitimized is thus subtly exposed.

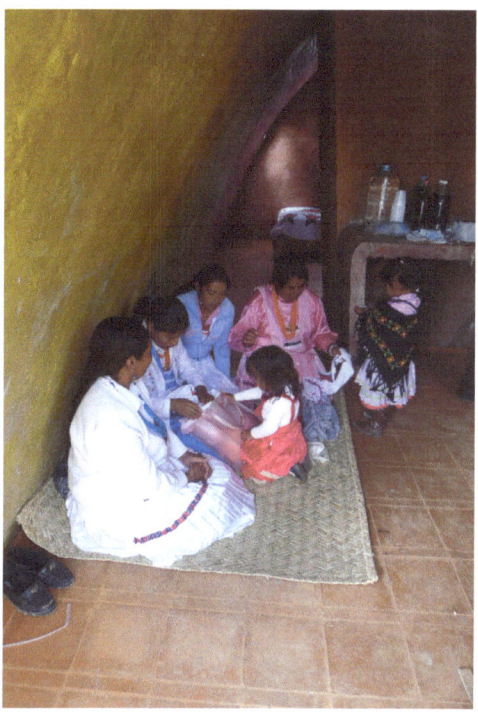

Figure 40 Interior, Trinidad Family House (Don Gregorio and Nicolasa), by Mobile Workshop Architects

Second, Jacob and Isaac see constraints as opportunities. They are interested not in high architecture, but in designing light-weight resilient structures that are not only affordable and easy to build but also satisfy cultural needs and desires (Smeke and Smeke, 2013a). This is accompanied by the realization that the creative act of design is now expanded to include the coordination of different disciplines and stakeholders in the construction of the house and the social and technological infrastructures that animate it. Designed as a linear layout (incorporating living spaces as well as spaces for animals and drying harvest) and enclosed in a self-supporting catenary shell, constructed out of 'lightweight structural panel with low density polyurethane infill' that achieves the ceiling height of 3.4 meters (Smeke and Smeke, 2013a). The dwelling is also an integrated unit. The axonometric view shows its conception as a *machine for living in*, where technology is not added to a static shell but is designed into the envelope. However, the house also responds to the 'metaphysical needs' of the people (Smeke and Smeke, 2013b). Jacob and Isaac suggest that instead of importing/imposing the frameworks of western domesticity and interiority, they have paid attention to domestic rituals and a bodily occupation of space—sitting on the floor on mats woven out of natural fibres, cooking in a specific way, valuing the use of natural colours, and not preferring to have large openings that may make the occupant feel exposed rather than protected. In other words, the dwelling brings together technical and cultural orientations. *Rural Habitat* is well timed for its audience in Sydney and at Customs House, as issues of social justice, and the global and ethical role of the architect is now becoming more prominent as a response to the increasing corporatization of the profession.

References

Australian Architecture Association. Who we Are. Available from: www.architecture.org.au/whoweare [Accessed 9 May 2014].

Clark J., Stead N., Burns K., Kaji-O'Grady S., Willis J., Roan A. and Matthewson G. (2014). Parlour: Women, Equity, Architecture. Available from: http://www.archiparlour.org/about/parlour [Accessed 9 May 2014].

Kaldor Art Projects. Available from: http://kaldorartprojects.org.au/project-archive/thomas-demand [Accessed 9 May 2014].

Smeke I. and Smeke J. (2013a). Interview. 29 August.

Smeke I. and Smeke J. (2013b). Text for Rural Habitat Exhibition.

N, (no date a), About. Available from: http://website-n.com/beyond/about.html [Accessed 9 May 2014].

N, (no date b), N1: How to be a Good Witness. Available from: http://website-n.com/n1/index.html [Accessed 9 May 2014].

N, (no date c), N3: Index Forum. Available from: http://website-n.com/n3/index.html [Accessed 9 May 2014].

N, (no date d), N4: Kaldor Public Art Projects, "The Dailies" by Thomas Demand. Available from: http://website-n.com/n4/index.html [Accessed 9 May 2014].

N, (no date e), N6: Audio Architecture: Dissonance Studio. Available from: http://website-n.com/n6/index.html [Accessed 9 May 2014].

Office for Good Design. http://7kindsofhappiness.com [Accessed 9 May 2014].

Super Sydney (2012). Available from: www.supersydney.org [Accessed 24 September].

Rivard T. (2013a). Exhibition Text.

Rivard T. (2013b). Interview. 15 March.

Taylor J. (2012). *The Third Landscape* [Catalog of an exhibition held at the Tin Sheds Gallery at University of Sydney for the Sydney Architecture Festival, 18 October to 17 November 2012] Sydney.

Practices Featured

Adam Jasper (Lecturer, School of Design, UTS)

Adrian Lahoud (Programme Leader, MArch Urban Design, The Bartlett, University College London)

Ann Quinlan (Senior Lecturer in Architecture at the Faculty of Built Environment, UNSW)

Anna Rubbo (Adjunct Senior Scholar Centre for Sustainable Urban Development, Earth Institute at Columbia University)

Anthony Burke (Professor of Architecture, UTS)

Aspect Studios

Brett Levy (General Manager National Indigenous Radio Service)

Carte Blanche (Sydney based collective of designers and architects)

Christopher Polly (Director of Christopher Polly Architect)

City of Sydney

Colin Stewart Architects

David Burns (Senior Lecturer, School of Design, UTS)

Department of Infrastructure and Regional Development, Australia

Edward Glaeser (Fred and Eleanor Glimp Professor of Economics, Harvard University)

Elizabeth Farelley (architectural critic, Sydney Morning Herald)

Gerard Reinmuth (Director of Terroir and Professor of Architecture, UTS)

Hannah Tribe (Director of Tribe Studio)

Historic Houses Trust (now part of Sydney Living Museums)

Holly Williams (Curator/Manager UTS ART)

Jacob Smeke Levy and Issac Smeke Levy (Directors, Mobile Workshop Architects)

The Japan Foundation Sydney

Jennifer Kwok (Manager of Customs House, Sydney)

Jennifer Turpin (Artist, Turpin+Crawford Studio, with an interest in kinetic public art installations)

LAVA Architects

Lisa McCutchion (Frasers Property)

M Hank Haeusler (Senior Lecturer in Architecture at the Faculty of Built Environment, UNSW)

Marion Weiss and Michael Manfredi (Weiss Manfredi)

Michaelie Crawford (Artist, Turpin+Crawford Studio, with an interest in kinetic public art installations)

Michael Neuman (Professor of Sustainable Urbanism at the Faculty of Built Environment, UNSW)

Michael Ripoll (Fine jeweller, silversmith, and member of The Society of Arts and Crafts of NSW, Australia)

New South Wales (NSW) Government

NSW Planning & Infrastructure

Open Agenda (University of Technology of Sydney, UTS)

Patrick Keane (Director, Enter Projects)

Peter Murphy (freelance photographer based in Sydney)

Philip Beesley (Professor, School of Architecture, University of Waterloo)

Reko Rennie (Indigenous artist based in Melbourne)

Sam Crawford (Director of Sam Crawford Architects)

Sam Marshall (Architect)

Stewart Hollenstein (Architectural practice in Sydney)

Tarsha Finney (Senior Lecturer in Architecture, UTS)

Tim Knowles (Award winning British artist)

Tim Vyse and Sam Westlake at Jane Irwin Landscape Architect, Australian Institute of Landscape Architects (AILA)

Sam Spurr (Research Fellow, School of Architecture and Built Environment, University of Adelaide)

Tim Williams (Architect and Urbanist, director and owner of Tim Williams Architects, co-curator and co-organizer of Super Sydney)

Tom Rivard (Director, Lean Productions, a multi-disciplinary practice)

Transport for NSW

Index

A

Aspect Studios, 42, 47

B

Beesley, Philip, 58, 64–66
Burns, David, 81, 82

C

Carte Blanche, 58, 60, 61
City of Sydney, 8, 10, 14–16, 24, 25
Colin Stewart Architects, 43, 44, 45
Collaborative practices, 80–85, 87–90, 92
Crawford, Sam, 25
Criticism, 24, 30, 32
Curating, 1, 2, 7, 9, 11, 13, 17–19
Customs House, 1, 2, 3, 6–9, 14

D

Density, 24, 25, 33, 36
Department of Infrastructure and Regional Development, Australia, 42, 46–48
Domesticity, 24, 25, 29, 35, 36

E

Edward Glaeser, 25, 32–34
Elizabeth Farrelly, 30–32

F

Finney, Tarsha, 25, 35

G

Gender, women, 80, 82–85

H

Haeusler, M Hank, 7
Historic Houses Trust, 24, 28, 29
Hypersurface, 6, 7

I

Immersive, 58, 59, 64, 66, 71, 72
Infrastructural topography, 36
Infrastructure, 24, 25, 27, 29, 33, 36, 37
Installation, 58, 59, 61–66, 75, 76
Interactive, 6, 7, 9

J

Japan Foundation Sydney, 11–13
Jasper, Adam, 17
Jennifer Kwok, 83

K

Keane, Patrick, 67, 69, 70
Knowles, Tim, 75–77

L

Lahoud, Adrian, 81, 82
Landscape urbanism, 42, 45, 46
LAVA Architects, 59, 68, 71–73
Liveability, liveable, 46, 52

M
Marshall, Sam, 30
McCutchion, Lisa, 49
Museum of Contemporary Art Australia (MCA), 30–32
Museum of Old and New Art in Tasmania (MONA), 17, 20

N
Neuman, Michael, 27, 28
New South Wales (NSW) Government, 50
NSW Planning & Infrastructure, 24, 32–34

O
Open Agenda, 6, 8

P
Polly, Christopher, 25, 26
Projective mapping, 80, 81, 85, 86, 88
Public art, 58, 59, 73, 75, 76

Q
Quinlan, Ann, 83

R
Rennie, Reko, 75–77
Ripoll, Michael, 3–6

Rivard, Tom, 80, 84–89
Rubbo, Anna, 14, 15

S
Smeke, Levy Jacob and Issac Smeke Levy, 90–93
Spurr, Sam, 81, 82
Stewart Hollenstein Architects, 43–45
Sydney Architecture Festival, 2, 6, 9

T
Transport for NSW, 51, 52
Transport, 46, 50–53
Tribe, Hannah, 29
Turpin and Crawford Studio, 73, 74
Tusculum, 24

U
University of New South Wales (UNSW), 2, 7, 9
University of Sydney, 24
University of Technology Sydney (UTS) 1, 2, 3, 8, 17, 25, 30, 35
Utzon Lecture Series, 36

W
Weiss Manfredi Architects, 36, 37
Williams, Holly, 17–20

www.ingramcontent.com/pod-product-compliance
Lightning Source LLC
Chambersburg PA
CBHW041432300426
44116CB00004B/47